Pericles Prince of Tyre

By William Shakespeare

Edited by Julien Coallier

Copyright Julien Coallier 2012

All Rights Reserved.

Scenes

Act I – 9

INTRO

Scene 1: A room in the palace. (Antioch)

Scene 2: A room in the palace. (Tyre)

Scene 3: An ante-chamber in the palace. (Tyre)

Scene 4: A room in the Governor's house. (Tarsus)

Act II – 35

Scene 1: An open place by the sea-side. (Pentapolis)

Scene 2: A public way or platform

Scene 3: A hall of state: a banquet prepared

Scene 4: A room in the Governor's house. (Tyre)

Scene 5: A room in the palace. (Pentapolis)

Act III – 63

INTRO

Scene 1: On ship.

Scene 2: A room in Cerimon's house. (Ephesus)

Scene 3: A room in Cleon's house. (Tarsus)

Scene 4: A room in Cerimon's house. (Ephesus)

Act IV – 81

INTRO

Scene 1: An open place near the sea-shore. (Tarsus)

Scene 2: A room in a brothel. (Mytilene)

Scene 3: A room in Cleon's house. (Tarsus)

Scene 4: Chorus.

Scene 5: A street before the brothel. (Mytilene)

Scene 6: A room in the brothel.

Act V – 113

INTRO

Scene 1: On board Pericles' ship, (off Mytilene)

Scene 2: Chorus.

Scene 3: The temple of Diana at Ephesus

Characters

All

Antiochus, king of Antioch

Bawd

Both

Boult (Pandar's servant)

Cerimon (A lord of Ephesus)

Cleon (Governor of Tarsus)

Diana (Daughter of Antiochus)

Dionyza (Wife to Cleon)

Escanes (A lord of Tyre)

First Fisherman

First Gentleman

First Knight

First Lord

First Pirate

First Sailor

First Servant

Gower (As chorus)

Helicanus (A lord of Tyre)

Knights

Leonine (Servant to Dionyza)

Lord

Lychorida (Nurse to Marina)

Lysimachus (Governor of Mytilene)

Marina (Daughter to Pericles and Thaisa)

Marshal

Messenger

Pandar

Pericles (Prince of Tyre)

Philemon (Servant to Cerimon)

Second Fisherman

Second Gentleman

Second Knight

Second Lord

Second Pirate

Second Sailor

Servant

Simonides (King of Pentapolis)

Thaisa (Daughter to Simonides)

Thaliard (A lord of Antioch)

Third Fisherman

Third Knight

Third Lord

Third Pirate

Tyrian Sailor

Act I, Intro

(**Gower** enters)

Gower: To sing a song that old was sung from ashes ancient Gower is come;

Assuming man's infirmities to glad your ear and please your eyes.

It hath been sung at festivals on ember-eves and holy-ales; and lords and ladies in their lives have read it for restoratives.

The purchase is to make men glorious; a cultivation of esteems in refinement of age, for the better as indeed

If you, born in these latter times, when wit's more ripe, accept my rhymes.

And that to hear an old man sing may to your wishes pleasure bring

Ay life would wish, and that I might waste it for you, like taper-light.

This Antioch, then, Antiochus the Great built up this city for his chiefest seat.

The fairest in all Syria, I tell you what mine authors say.

This king unto him took a brother who died and left a female heir.

So buxom, blithe, and full of face as heaven had lent her all his grace.

With whom the father liking took and her to incest did provoke.

Bad child, worse father! To entice his own to evil should be done by none.

Custom what they did begin was with long use account no sin.

The beauty of this sinful dame made many princes thither frame to seek her as a bed-fellow; in marriage-pleasures play-fellow.

Which to prevent he made a law to keep her still, and men in awe, that whoso asked her for his wife his riddle told not, lost his life.

So for her many a weight did die, as yon grim looks do testify.

What now ensues, to the judgment of your eye I give my cause who best can justify.

(Exits)

Act I, Scene 1

A room in the palace. (Antioch)

(Antiochus, Prince Pericles, and followers enter)

Antiochus: Young prince of Tyre, you have at large received the danger of the task you undertake.

Pericles: I have, Antiochus, and, with a soul emboldened with the glory of her praise, think death no hazard in this enterprise.

Antiochus: Bring in our daughter, clothed like a bride, for the embracements even of Jupiter himself; at whose conception till Lucina reigned.

Nature this dowry gave, to glad her presence, the senate-house of planets all did sit to knit in her their best perfections.

(Music)

(The Daughter of Antiochus enters)

Pericles: See where she comes, apparelled like the spring, graces her subjects and her thoughts the king of every virtue gives renown to men!

Her face the book of praises, where is read nothing but curious pleasures, as from thence sorrow were ever razed and testy wrath could never be her mild companion.

You gods that made me man, and sway in love that have inflamed desire in my breast to taste the fruit of yon celestial tree, or die in the adventure, be my helps, as I am son and servant to your will; to compass such a boundless happiness!

Antiochus: Prince Pericles…

Pericles: That would be son to great Antiochus.

Antiochus: Before thee stands this fair Hesperides, with golden fruit but dangerous to be touched, for death-like dragons here affright thee hard.

Her face, like heaven, enticeth thee to vie.

Her countless glory, which desert must gain, and which without desert, because thine eye presumes to reach, all thy whole heap must die.

Yon sometimes famous princes, like thyself, drawn by report, adventurous by desire; tell thee with speechless tongues and semblance pale that without covering save yon field of stars.

Here they stand martyrs, slain in Cupid's wars, and with dead cheeks advise thee to desist for going on death's net, whom none resist.

Pericles: Antiochus, I thank thee, who hath taught my frail mortality to know itself, and by those fearful objects to prepare this body, like to them to what I must; for death remembered should be like a mirror who tells us life's but breath, to trust it error.

I'll make my will then and as sick men do who know the world, see heaven, but feeling woe gripe not at earthly joys as erst they did; so I bequeath a happy peace to you and all good men as every prince should do.

My riches to the earth from whence they came, but my unspotted fire of love to you.

(To the Daughter of Antiochus)

Thus ready for the way of life or death, I wait the sharpest blow, Antiochus.

Antiochus: Scorning advice, read the conclusion then, which read and not expounded, this decreed, as these before thee thou thyself shalt bleed.

Daughter of Antiochus: Of all say'd yet, mayst thou prove prosperous!

Of all said, yet, I wish thee happiness!

Pericles: Like a bold champion, I assume the lists,

Nor ask advice of any other thought

But faithfulness and courage. 110

(He reads the riddle)

I am no viper, yet I feed on mother's flesh which did me breed.

I sought a husband, in which labour I found that kindness in a father.

He's father, son, and husband mild; I mother, wife, and yet his child.

How they may be, and yet in two, as you will live resolve it you.

Sharp physic is the last, but oh you powers that give heaven countless eyes to view men's acts; why cloud they not their sights perpetually, if this be true, which makes me pale to read it?

Fair glass of light, I loved you, and could still,

(Takes hold of the hand of the Daughter of Antiochus)

Were not this glorious casket stored with ill, but I must tell you, now my thoughts revolt for he's no man on whom perfections wait; that knowing sin within will touch the gate.

You are a fair viol, and your sense the strings; who fingered to make man his lawful music would draw heaven down, and all the gods, to hearken.

Being plae'd upon before your time, hell only danceth at so harsh a chime.

Good sooth, I care not for you.

Antiochus: Prince Pericles, touch not upon thy life for that's an article within our law as dangerous as the rest.

Your time's expired, either expound now, or receive your sentence.

Pericles: Great king, few love to hear the sins they love to act, it would braid yourself too near for me to tell it.

Who has a book of all that monarchs do, he's more secure to keep it shut than shown for vice repeated is like the wandering wind.

Blows dust in other's eyes, to spread itself, and yet the end of all is bought thus dear, the breath is gone, and the sore eyes see clear.

To stop the air would hurt them.

The blind mole casts copped hills towards heaven to tell the earth is thronged by man's oppression, and the poor worm doth die for it.

Kings are earth's gods in vice their law's their will, and if Jupiter stray who dares say Jupiter doth ill?

It is enough you know, and it is fit; what being more known grows worse, to smother it.

All love the womb that their first being bred, then give my tongue like leave to love my head.

Antiochus: (From Aside) Heaven, that I had thy head! He has found the meaning, but I will gloze with him.

Young prince of Tyre, though by the tenor of our strict edict, your exposition misinterpreting, we might proceed to cancel of your days; yet hope succeeding from so fair a tree as your fair self, doth tune us otherwise.

Forty days longer we do respite you, if by which time our secret be undone, this mercy shows we'll joy in such a son.

Until then your entertain shall be as doth befit our honour and your worth.

(Exeunt all but Pericles)

Pericles: How courtesy would seem to cover sin, when what is done is like a hypocrite, the which is good in nothing but in sight!

If it be true that I interpret false, then were it certain you were not so bad as with foul incest to abuse your soul; where now you're both a father and a son by your untimely claspings with your child which pleasure fits a husband, not a father.

She an eater of her mother's flesh, by the defiling of her parent's bed and both like serpents are, who though they feed on sweetest flowers, yet they poison breed.

Antioch, farewell! For wisdom sees those men blush not in actions blacker than the night will shun no course to keep them from the light.

One sin, I know, another doth provoke; murder's as near to lust as flame to smoke.

Poison and treason are the hands of sin, ay, and the targets to put off the shame.

Then, lest my lie be cropped to keep you clear by flight I'll shun the danger which I fear.

(Exits)

(Antiochus re-enters)

Antiochus: He hath found the meaning, for which we mean to have his head.

He must not live to trumpet forth my infamy, nor tell the world Antiochus doth sin in such a loathed manner; and therefore instantly this prince must die.

For by his fall my honour must keep high.

Who attends us there?

(Thaliard enters)

Thaliard: Doth your highness call?

Antiochus: Thaliard,

You are of our chamber, and our mind partakes her private actions to your secrecy; and for your faithfulness we will advance you.

Thaliard, behold here's poison and here's gold, we hate the prince of Tyre and thou must kill him.

It fits thee not to ask the reason why, because we bid it.

Say, is it done?

Thaliard: My lord, it is done.

Antiochus: Enough.

(A Messenger enters)

Let your breath cool yourself, telling your haste.

Messenger: My lord, prince Pericles is fled.

(Exits)

Antiochus: As thou wilt live, fly after; and like an arrow shot from a well-experienced archer hits the mark.

His eye doth level at, so thou never return unless thou say: Prince Pericles is dead.

Thaliard: My lord, if I can get him within my pistol's length, I'll make him sure enough.

So, farewell to your highness.

Antiochus: Thaliard, adieu!

(Thaliard exits)

Till Pericles be dead, my heart can lend no succor to my head.

(Exits)

Act I, Scene 2

A room in the palace. (Tyre)

(Pericles enters)

Pericles: (To Lords without) Let none disturb us.

Why should this change of thoughts, the sad companion, dull-eyed melancholy; be my so used a guest as not an hour in the day's glorious walk, or peaceful night the tomb where grief should sleep, can breed me quiet?

Here pleasures court mine eyes, and mine eyes shun them and danger, which I feared is at Antioch, whose aim seems far too short to hit me here.

Yet neither pleasure's art can joy my spirits, nor yet the other's distance comfort me.

Then it is thus, the passions of the mind that have their first conception by mis-dread have after-nourishment and life by care; and what was first but fear what might be done grows elder now and cares it be not done.

So with me, the great Antiochus, against whom I am too little to contend, since he's so great can make his will his act will think me speaking; though I swear to silence nor boots it me to say I honour him.

If he suspect I may dishonour him and what may make him blush in being known, he'll stop the course by which it might be known; with hostile forces he'll overspread the land, and with the instant of war will look so huge, Amazement shall drive courage from the state.

Our men be vanquished ere they do resist and subjects punished that never thought offence; which care of them, not pity of myself, who am no more but as the tops of tree.

Which fence the roots they grow by and defend them makes both my body pine and soul to languish and punish that before that he would punish.

(Helicanus enters with other Lords)

First Lord: Joy and all comfort in your sacred breast!

Second Lord: And keep your mind, till you return to us, peaceful and comfortable!

Helicanus: Peace, peace, and give experience tongue.

They do abuse the king that flatter him, for flattery is the bellows blows up sin; the thing which is flattered, but a spark to which that blast gives heat and stronger glowing; whereas reproof obedient and in order fits kings, as they are men, for they may error.

When Signior Sooth here does proclaim a peace, he flatters you, makes war upon your life.

Prince, pardon me, or strike me, if you please; I cannot be much lower than my knees.

Pericles: All leave us else; but let your cares overlook what shipping and what lading's in our haven, and then return to us.

(Exeunt Lords)

Helicanus, thou hast moved us: what seest thou in our looks?

Helicanus: An angry brow, dread lord.

Pericles: If there be such a dart in princes' frowns, how durst thy tongue move anger to our face?

Helicanus: How dare the plants look up to heaven, from whence they have their nourishment?

Pericles: Thou know'st I have power to take thy life from thee.

Helicanus: (Kneeling)

I have ground the axe myself, do you but strike the blow.

Pericles: Rise, pray to thee, rise. sit down.

Thou art no flatterer.

I thank thee for it; and heaven forbid that kings should let their ears hear their faults hid!

Fit counsellor and servant for a prince, who by thy wisdom makest a prince thy servant; what wouldst thou have me do?

Helicanus: To bear with patience such griefs as you yourself do lay upon yourself.

Pericles: Thou speak'st like a physician, Helicanus, that minister'st a potion unto me that thou wouldst tremble to receive thyself.

Attend me, then.

I went to Antioch where as thou know'st, against the face of death, I sought the purchase of a glorious beauty.

From whence an issue I might propagate, are arms to princes and bring joys to subjects.

Her face was to mine eye beyond all wonder; the rest hark in thine ear, as black as incest.

By my knowledge found, the sinful father seemed not to strike, but was smooth, but thou know'st this, it is time to fear when tyrants seem to kiss.

Such fear so grew in me, I hither fled under the covering of a careful night who seemed my good protector; and, being here; bethought me what was past, what might succeed.

I knew him tyrannous; and tyrants' fears decrease not, but grow faster than the years; and should he doubt it; as no doubt he doth that I should open to the listening air how many worthy princes' bloods were shed to keep his bed of blackness unlaid open to top that doubt, he'll fill this land with arms and make pretense of wrong that I have done him.

When all, for mine, if I may call offence, must feel war's blow who spares not innocence.

Which love to all of which thyself art one who now reprovest me for it…

Helicanus: Alas, sir!

Pericles: Drew sleep out of mine eyes, blood from my cheeks, musings into my mind, with thousand doubt show I might stop this tempest ere it came; and finding little comfort to relieve them, I thought it princely charity to grieve them.

Helicanus: Well, my lord, since you have given me leave to speak.

Freely will I speak.

Antiochus you fear, and justly too, I think, you fear the tyrant who either by public war or private treason will take away your life.

Therefore, my lord, go travel for a while, till that his rage and anger be forgot, or till the Destinies do cut his thread of life.

Your rule direct to any; if to me.

Day serves not light more faithful than I'll be.

Pericles: I do not doubt thy faith;

But should he wrong my liberties in my absence?

Helicanus: We'll mingle our bloods together in the earth, from whence we had our being and our birth.

Pericles: Tyre, I now look from thee then, and to Tarsus intend my travel, where I'll hear from thee; and by whose letters I'll dispose myself.

The care I had and have of subjects' good, on thee I lay whose wisdom's strength can bear it.

I'll take thy word for faith, not ask thine oath who shuns not to break one will sure crack both, but in our orbs we'll live so round and safe, that time of both this truth shall never convince; thou show'dst a subject's shine, I a true prince.

(Exeunt)

Act I, Scene 3

An ante-chamber in the palace. (Tyre)

(Thaliard enters)

Thaliard: So, this is Tyre, and this the court.

Here must I kill King Pericles, and if I do it not I am sure to be hanged at home.

It is dangerous.

Well, I perceive he was a wise fellow, and had good discretion that, being bid to ask what he would of the king, desired he might know none of his secrets.

Now do I see he had some reason for it, for if a king bid a man be a villain, he's bound by the indenture of his oath to be one!

Hush! here come the lords of Tyre.

(Helicanus and Escanes, with other Lords of Tyre enters)

Helicanus: You shall not need, my fellow peers of Tyre, further to question me of your king's departure.

His sealed commission left in trust with me, doth speak sufficiently he's gone to travel.

Thaliard: (From Aside) How! The king gone!

Helicanus: If further yet you will be satisfied, why as it were unlicensed of your loves, he would depart, I'll give some light unto you.

Being at Antioch…

Thaliard: (From Aside) What from Antioch?

Helicanus: Royal Antiochus, on what cause I know not, took some displeasure at him; at least he judged so.

Doubting lest that he had errored or sinned to show his sorrow, he would correct himself; so puts himself unto the shipman's toil, with whom each minute threatens life or death.

Thaliard: (From Aside) Well, I perceive I shall not be hanged now, although I would; but since he's gone, the king's seas must please.

He escaped the land, to perish at the sea.

I'll present myself.

Peace to the lords of Tyre!

Helicanus: Lord Thaliard from Antiochus is welcome.

Thaliard: From him I come with message unto princely Pericles, but since my landing I have understood your lord has betook himself to unknown travels; my message must return from whence it came.

Helicanus: We have no reason to desire it, commended to our master, not to us.

Yet, were you shall depart, this we desire as friends to Antioch, we may feast in Tyre.

(Exeunt)

Act I, Scene 4

A room in the Governor's house. (Tarus)

(Cleon, the governor of Tarsus, with Dionyza, and others enter)

Cleon: My Dionyza, shall we rest us here, and by relating tales of others' griefs see if it will teach us to forget our own?

Dionyza: That were to blow at fire in hope to quench it, for who digs hills because they do aspire throws down one mountain to cast up a higher.

Oh my distressed lord, even such our griefs are, here they're but felt, and seen with mischief's eyes, but like to groves being topped, they higher rise.

Cleon: Oh Dionyza, who wanteth food, and will not say he wants it, or can conceal his hunger till he famish?

Our tongues and sorrows do sound deep our woes into the air; our eyes do weep, till tongues fetch breath that may proclaim them louder; that if heaven slumber while their creatures want, they may awake their helps to comfort them.

I'll then discourse our woes, felt several years, and wanting breath to speak help me with tears.

Dionyza: I'll do my best, sir.

Cleon: This Tarsus, over which I have the government, a city on whom plenty held full hand for riches strewed herself even in the streets; whose towers bore heads so high they kissed the clouds and strangers never beheld, but wondered at whose men and dames so jetted and adorned like one another's glass to trim them by.

Their tables were stored full, to glad the sight and not so much to feed on as delight; all poverty was scorned, and pride so great the name of help grew odious to repeat.

Dionyza: Oh it is too true.

Cleon: See what heaven can do! By this our change, these mouths who but of late, earth, sea, and air, were all too little to content and please.

Although they gave their creatures in abundance, as houses are defiled for want of use; they are now starved for want of exercise.

Those palates who, not yet two summers younger must have inventions to delight the taste would now be glad of bread, and beg for it.

Those mothers who, to nousle up their babes, thought nought too curious are ready now to eat those little darlings whom they loved.

So sharp are hunger's teeth, that man and wife draw lots who first shall die to lengthen life.

Here stands a lord, and there a lady weeping, here many sink, yet those which see them fall have scarce strength left to give them burial.

Is not this true?

Dionyza: Our cheeks and hollow eyes do witness it.

Cleon: Oh let those cities that of plenty's cup and her prosperities so largely taste with their superfluous riots, hear these tears!

The misery of Tarsus may be theirs.

(A Lord enters)

Lord: Where's the lord governor?

Cleon: Here.

Speak out thy sorrows which thou bring'st in haste, for comfort is too far for us to expect.

Lord: We have descried, upon our neighbouring shore, a portly sail of ships make hitherward.

Cleon: I thought as much.

One sorrow never comes but brings an heir that may succeed as his inheritor; and so in ours some neighbouring nation taking advantage of our misery hath stuffed these hollow vessels, with their power to beat us down.

The which are down already and make a conquest of unhappy me, whereas no glory's got to overcome.

Lord: That's the least fear; for, by the semblance

Of their white flags displayed, they bring us peace and come to us as favourers, not as foes.

Cleon: Thou speak'st like him's untutored to repeat.

Who makes the fairest show means most deceit but bring they what they will and what they can, what need we fear?

The ground's the lowest, and we are half way there.

Go tell their general we attend him here to know for what he comes, and whence he comes and what he craves.

Lord: I go, my lord.

(Exits)

Cleon: Welcome is peace, if he on peace consist, if wars we are unable to resist.

(Pericles enters with Attendants)

Pericles: Lord governor, for so we hear you are, let not our ships and number of our men be like a beacon fired to amaze your eyes.

We have heard your miseries as far as Tyre and seen the desolation of your streets.

Nor come we to add sorrow to your tears, but to relieve them of their heavy load; and these our ships you happily may think are like the Trojan horse was stuffed within.

With bloody veins, expecting overthrow are stored with corn to make your needy bread and give them life whom hunger starved half dead.

All: The gods of Greece protect you! And we'll pray for you.

Pericles: Arise, I pray you, rise.

We do not look for reverence, but to love.

Harbourage for ourself, our ships, and men.

Cleon: The which when any shall not gratify or pay you with unthankfulness in thought.

Be it our wives, our children, or ourselves the curse of heaven and men succeed their evils!

Till when, the which I hope shall never be seen, your grace is welcome to our town and us.

Pericles: Which welcome we'll accept; feast here awhile **until** our stars that frown lend us a smile.

(Exeunt)

Act II, Scene 1

An open place by the sea-side. (Pentapolis)

(Pericles enter wet)

Pericles: Yet cease your ire, you angry stars of heaven!

Wind, rain, and thunder, remember, earthly man is but a substance that must yield to you; and I, as fits my nature, do obey you.

Alas, the sea hath cast me on the rocks, washed me from shore to shore and left me breath.

Nothing to think on but ensuing death, let it suffice the greatness of your powers to have bereft a prince of all his fortunes; and having thrown him from your watery grave, here to have death in peace is all he'll crave.

(Three Fisherman enter)

First Fisherman: What, oh, Pilch!

Second Fisherman: Ha, come and bring away the nets!

First Fisherman: What, Patch-breech, I say!

Third Fisherman: What say you, master?

First Fisherman: Look how thou stirrest now! Come away, or I'll fetch thee with a wanion.

Third Fisherman: Faith, master, I am thinking of the poor men that were cast away before us even now.

First Fisherman: Alas, poor souls, it grieved my heart to hear what pitiful cries they made to us to help them, when, well-a-day, we could scarce help ourselves.

Third Fisherman: Nay, master, said not I as much when I saw the porpus, how he bounced and tumbled?

They say they're half fish, half flesh.

A plague on them, they never come but I look to be washed.

Master, I marvel how the fishes live in the sea.

First Fisherman: Why, as men do a-land; the great ones eat up the little ones.

I can compare our rich misers to nothing so fitly as to a whale, all plays and tumbles, driving the poor fry before him, and at last devours them all at a mouthful.

Such whales have I heard on o' the land, who never leave gaping till they've swallowed the whole parish, church, steeple, bells, and all.

Pericles: (From Aside) A pretty moral.

Third Fisherman: Master, if I had been the sexton, I would have been that day in the belfry.

Second Fisherman: Why, man?

Third Fisherman: Because he should have swallowed me too: and when I had been in his belly, I would have kept such a jangling of the bells that he should never have left, till he cast bells, steeple, church, and parish up again.

If the good King Simonides were of my mind…

Pericles: (From Aside) Simonides!

Third Fisherman: We would purge the land of these drones, that rob the bee of her honey.

Pericles: (From Aside) How from the finny subject of the sea, these fishers tell the infirmities of men; and from their watery empire recollect all that may men approve or men detect!

Peace be at your labour, honest fishermen.

Second Fisherman: Honest! Good fellow, what's that?

If it be a day fits you, search out of the calendar, and nobody look after it.

Pericles: May see the sea hath cast upon your coast.

Second Fisherman: What a drunken knave was the sea to cast thee in our way!

Pericles: A man whom both the waters and the wind, in that vast tennis-court, have made the ball for them to play upon, entreats you pity him.

He asks of you, that never used to beg.

First Fisherman: No, friend, cannot you beg? Here's them in our country Greece gets more with begging than we can do with working.

Second Fisherman: Canst thou catch any fishes, then?

Pericles: I never practised it.

Second Fisherman: Nay, then thou wilt starve, sure; for here's nothing to be got now-a-days, unless thou canst fish for it.

Pericles: What I have been I have forgot to know, but what I am, want teaches me to think on.

A man thronged up with cold, my veins are chill and have no more of life than may suffice to give my tongue that heat to ask your help; which if you shall refuse, when I am dead for that I am a man, pray see me buried.

First Fisherman: Die quoth I? Now gods forbid! I have a gown here; come, put it on; keep thee warm.

Now, before me, a handsome fellow! Come, thou shalt go home, and we'll have flesh for holidays, fish for fasting-days and moreover puddings and flap-jacks, and thou shalt be welcome.

Pericles: I thank you, sir.

Second Fisherman: Hark you, my friend; you said you could not beg.

Pericles: I did but crave.

Second Fisherman: But crave! Then I'll turn craver too, and so I shall escape whipping.

Pericles: Why, are all your beggars whipped, then?

Second Fisherman: Oh not all, my friend, not all, for if all your beggars were whipped, I would wish no better office than to be beadle; but master, I'll go draw up the net.

(Exits with Third Fisherman)

Pericles: (From Aside) How well this honest mirth becomes their labour!

First Fisherman: Hark you, sir, do you know where ye are?

Pericles: Not well.

First Fisherman: Why I'll tell you, this is called Pentapolis and our king the good Simonides.

Pericles: The good King Simonides, do you call him.

First Fisherman: Ay sir, and he deserves so to be called for his peaceable reign and good government.

Pericles: He is a happy king, since he gains from his subjects the name of good by his government.

How far is his court distant from this shore?

First Fisherman: Marry, sir, half a day's journey, and I'll tell you he hath a fair daughter, and to-morrow is her birth-day; and there are princes and knights come from all parts of the world to just and tourney for her love.

Pericles: Were my fortunes equal to my desires, I could wish to make one there.

First Fisherman: Oh sir, things must be as they may and what a man cannot get, he may lawfully deal for his wife's soul.

(Second and Third Fishermen re-enter drawing up a net)

Second Fisherman: Help, master, help! Here's a fish hangs in the net like a poor man's right in the law; it will hardly come out.

Ha! bots on it, it is come at last, and it is turned to a rusty armour.

Pericles: An armour, friends! I pray you, let me see it.

Thanks, fortune, yet, that, after all my crosses, thou givest me somewhat to repair myself; and though it was mine own, part of my heritage which my dead father did bequeath to me.

With this strict charge, even as he left his life, keep it, my Pericles; it hath been a shield twist me and death.

Pointed to this brace, for that it saved me, keep it; in like necessity the which the gods protect thee from! May defend thee.

It kept where I kept, I so dearly loved it; till the rough seas that spare not any man took it in rage.

Though calmed have given it again.

I thank thee for it; my shipwreck know's no ill since I have here my father's gift in's will.

First Fisherman: What mean you, sir?

Pericles: To beg of you, kind friends, this coat of worth, for it was sometime target to a king; I know it by this mark.

He loved me dearly, and for his sake I wish the having of it; and that you would guide me to your sovereign's court where with it I may appear a gentleman.

If that ever my low fortune's better, I'll pay your bounties; till then rest your debtor.

First Fisherman: Why, wilt thou tourney for the lady?

Pericles: I'll show the virtue I have borne in arms.

First Fisherman: Why, do 'e take it, and the gods give thee good on it!

Second Fisherman: Ay, but hark you, my friend, it was we that made up this garment through the rough seams of the waters.

There are certain condolements, certain vails.

I hope, sir, if you thrive, you'll remember from whence you had it.

Pericles: Believe it, I will.

By your furtherance I am clothed in steel, and spite of all the rapture of the sea; this jewel holds his building on my arm.

Unto thy value I will mount myself upon a courser, whose delightful steps shall make the gazer joy to see him tread.

Only, my friend, I yet am unprovided of a pair of bases.

Second Fisherman: We'll sure provide: thou shalt have my best gown to make thee a pair; and I'll bring thee to the court myself.

Pericles: Then honour be but a goal to my will, this day I'll rise, or else add ill to ill.

(Exeunt)

Act II, Scene 2

A public way or platform leading to the lists.

(A pavilion by the side of it for the reception of King, Princess, Lords and company)

(Simonides, Thaisa, Lords, and Attendants enter)

Simonides: Are the knights ready to begin the triumph?

First Lord: They are, my liege, and stay your coming to present themselves.

Simonides: Return them, we are ready; and our daughter in honour of whose birth these triumphs are; sits here like beauty's child whom nature gat for men to see, and seeing wonder at.

(A Lord exits)

Thaisa: It pleaseth you, my royal father, to express my commendations great, whose merit's less.

Simonides: It's fit it should be so, for princes are a model which heaven makes like to itself.

As jewels lose their glory if neglected, so princes their renowns if not respected.

It is now your honour, daughter, to explain the labour of each knight in his device.

Thaisa: Which, to preserve mine honour, I'll perform.

(A Knight enters, he passes over and his Squire and presents his shield to the Princess)

Simonides: Who is the first that doth prefer himself?

Thaisa: A knight of Sparta, my renowned father and the device he bears upon his shield is a black Ethiope reaching at the sun, with the words: Your light is my life.

Simonides: He loves you well that holds his life of you.

(The Second Knight passes over)

Who is the second that presents himself?

Thaisa: A prince of Macedon, my royal father, and the device he bears upon his shield

Is an armed knight that's conquered by a lady;

The motto thus, in Spanish: I am one trusted to keep secrets.

(The Third Knight passes over)

Simonides: And what's the third?

Thaisa: The third of Antioch and his device, a wreath of chivalry; the words: The desire of glory has carried me.

(The Fourth Knight passes over)

Simonides: What is the fourth?

Thaisa: A burning torch that's turned upside down, the words: What feeds me, extinguishes me.

Simonides: Which shows that beauty hath his power and will, which can as well inflame as it can kill.

(The Fifth Knight passes over)

Thaisa: The fifth hand environed with clouds, holding out gold that's by the touchstone tried, the motto thus: Faith is to be tried.

(The Sixth Knight, Pericles, passes over)

Simonides: And what's the sixth and last, the which the knight himself with such a graceful courtesy delivered?

Thaisa: He seems to be a stranger; but his present is a withered branch, that's only green at top, the motto being: Is this hope I live striving for.

Simonides: A pretty moral from the dejected state wherein he is; he hopes by you his fortunes yet may flourish.

First Lord: He had need mean better than his outward show can any way speak in his just commend; for by his rusty outside he appears to have practised more the whipstock than the lance.

Second Lord: He well may be a stranger, for he comes to an honoured triumph strangely furnished.

Third Lord: And on set purpose let his armour rust until this day to scour it in the dust.

Simonides: Opinion's but a fool, that makes us scan the outward habit by the inward man;

but stay, the knights are coming.

We will withdraw into the gallery.

(Exeunt)

(Great shouts within and all cry: The mean knight!)

Act II, Scene 3

A hall of state: a banquet prepared.

(Simonides, Thaisa, Lords, Attendants, and Knights enter from tilting)

Simonides: Knights, to say you're welcome were superfluous.

To place upon the volume of your deeds, as in a title-page, your worth in arms were more than you expect, or more than his fit; since every worth in show commends itself.

Prepare for mirth, for mirth becomes a feast, you are princes and my guests.

Thaisa: You, my knight and guest, to whom this wreath of victory I give, and crown you king of this day's happiness.

Pericles: It is more by fortune, lady, than by merit.

Simonides: Call it by what you will, the day is yours, and here I hope is none that envies it.

In framing an artist, art hath thus decreed to make some good, but others to exceed; and you are her laboured scholar.

Come, queen of the feast…

For, daughter, so you are, here take your place.

Marshal the rest, as they deserve their grace.

Knights: We are honoured much by good Simonides.

Simonides: Your presence glads our days: honour we love, for who hates honour hates the gods above.

Marshal: Sir, yonder is your place.

Pericles: Some other is more fit.

First Knight: Contend not, sir, for we are gentlemen that neither in our hearts nor outward eyes envy the great nor do the low despise.

Pericles: You are right courteous knights.

Simonides: Sit, sir, sit.

Pericles: By Jupiter, I wonder, that is king of thoughts; these crates resist me, she but thought upon.

Thaisa: By Juno, that is queen of marriage, all meats that I eat do seem unsavoury.

Wishing him my meat, sure he's a gallant gentleman.

Simonides: He's but a country gentleman; has done no more than other knights have done, has broken a staff or so; so let it pass.

Thaisa: To me he seems like diamond to glass.

Pericles: Yon king's to me like to my father's picture, which tells me in that glory once he was; had princes sit like stars, about his throne and he the sun, for them to reverence.

None that beheld him, but like lesser lights did vail their crowns to his supremacy.

Where now his son's like a glow-worm in the night, the which hath fire in darkness, none in light.

Whereby I see that Time's the king of men, he's both their parent, and he is their grave, and gives them what he will, not what they crave.

Simonides: What, are you merry, knights?

Knights: Who can be other in this royal presence?

Simonides: Here, with a cup that's stored unto the brim, as you do love, fill to your mistress' lips.

We drink this health to you.

Knights: We thank your grace.

Simonides: Yet pause awhile, yon knight doth sit too melancholy, as if the entertainment in our court had not a show might countervail his worth.

Note it not you, Thaisa?

Thaisa: What is it to me, my father?

Simonides: Oh attend, my daughter.

Princes in this should live like gods above, who freely give to everyone that comes to honour them; and princes not doing so are like to gnats, which make a sound, but kill'd are wondered at.

Therefore to make his entrance more sweet, here, say we drink this standing-bowl of wine to him.

Thaisa: Alas, my father, it befits not me unto a stranger knight to be so bold.

He may my proffer take for an offence, since men take women's gifts for impudence.

Simonides: How! Do as I bid you, or you'll move me else.

Thaisa: (From Aside) Now, by the gods, he could not please me better.

Simonides: And furthermore tell him, we desire to know of him, of whence he is, his name and parentage.

Thaisa: The king my father, sir, has drunk to you.

Pericles: I thank him.

Thaisa: Wishing it so much blood unto your life.

Pericles: I thank both him and you, and pledge him freely.

Thaisa: And further he desires to know of you, of whence you are, your name and parentage.

Pericles: A gentleman of Tyre, my name Pericles, my education been in arts and arms who looking for adventures in the world was by the rough seas reft of ships and men; and after shipwreck driven upon this shore.

Thaisa: He thanks your grace; names himself Pericles, a gentleman of Tyre who only by misfortune of the seas bereft of ships and men, cast on this shore.

Simonides: Now, by the gods, I pity his misfortune, and will awake him from his melancholy.

Come, gentlemen, we sit too long on trifles and waste the time, which looks for other revels.

Even in your armours, as you are addressed will very well become a soldier's dance.

I will not have excuse, with saying this loud music is too harsh for ladies' heads, since they love men in arms as well as beds.

(The Knights dance)

So, this was well asked, it was so well performed.

Come, sir;

Here is a lady that wants breathing too, and I have heard you knights of Tyre are excellent in making ladies trip; and that their measures are as excellent.

Pericles: In those that practise them they are, my lord.

Simonides: Oh that's as much as you would be denied of your fair courtesy.

(The Knights and Ladies dance)

Unclasp, unclasp.

Thanks, gentlemen, to all; all have done well.

(To Pericles)

Be you at your best, Pages and lights to conduct these knights unto their several lodgings!

(To Pericles)

Yours sir, we have given order to be next our own.

Pericles: I am at your grace's pleasure.

Simonides: Princes, it is too late to talk of love, and that's the mark I know you level at; therefore each one betake him to his rest tomorrow all for speeding do their best.

(Exeunt)

Act II, Scene 4

A room in the Governor's house. (Tyre)

(Gower enters)

Gower: Here have you seen a mighty king, his child I wish to bring away from incest onto a better prince and benign lord that will prove awful both in deed and word.

Be quiet then as men should be, till he hath passed necessity.

I'll show you those in troubles reign, losing a mite, a mountain gain.

The good in conversation, to whom I give my benison is still at Tarsus, where each man thinks all is writ he speaking can and to remember what he does build his statue to make him glorious; but tidings to the contrary are brought your eyes.

What need speak I?

(At one door Pericles enters talking with Cleon, all the entourage enter with them)

(At another door a gentleman with a letter to Pericles; Pericles shows the letter to Cleon, gives the Messenger a reward and grants him leave.

(Pericles exits at one door and Cleon at another)

Gower: Good Helicane that stayed at home not to eat honey like a drone from others' labours; for though he strive to kill bad and keep good alive.

To fulfil his prince' desire, he sends word of all that happens in Tyre, how Thaliard came full bent with sin and had intent to murder him; and that in Tarsus was not best longer for him to make his rest.

He, doing so, put forth to seas where men have been; there's seldom ease, for now the wind begins to blow thunder above and deeps below, making such unquiet, that the ship should house him safe is wrecked and split.

He, good prince, having all lost by waves from coast to coast is toast.

All perishen of man, of pelf, he naught escaped but himself; till fortune were tired with doing bad, threw him ashore to give him glad.

Here he comes, what shall be next; pardon this old Gower, this longs the text.

(Exits)

(Helicanus and Escanes enter)

Helicanus: No, Escanes, know this of me, Antiochus from incest lived not free.

For which, the most high gods not minding longer to withhold the vengeance that they had in store, due to this heinous capital offence.

Even in the height and pride of all his glory, when he was seated in a chariot of an inestimable value, and his daughter with him.

A fire from heaven came and shrivelled up their bodies, even to loathing; for they so stunk that all those eyes adored them were at their fall.

Scorn now their hand should give them burial.

Escanes: It was very strange.

Helicanus: And yet but justice, for though this king were great, his greatness was no guard to bar heaven's shaft, but sin had his reward.

Escanes: It is very true.

(Two or three Lords enter)

First Lord: See, not a man in private conference or council has respect with him but he.

Second Lord: It shall no longer grieve without reproof.

Third Lord: And cursed be he that will not second it.

First Lord: Follow me then, Lord Helicane, a word.

Helicanus: With me? And welcome.

Happy day, my lords.

First Lord: Know that our griefs are risen to the top and now at length they overflow their banks.

Helicanus: Your griefs! For what? Wrong not your prince you love.

First Lord: Wrong not yourself then noble Helicane, but if the prince do live let us salute him, or know what ground's made happy by his breath.

If in the world he live, we'll seek him out, if in his grave he rest, we'll find him there and be resolved he lives to govern us; or dead, give's cause to mourn his funeral and leave us to our free election.

Second Lord: Whose death indeed's the strongest in our censure, and knowing this kingdom is without a head…

Like goodly buildings left without a roof soon fall to ruin, your noble self, that best know how to rule and how to reignl; we thus submit unto our sovereign.

All: Live, noble Helicane!

Helicanus: For honour's cause, forbear your suffrages.

If that you love Prince Pericles, forbear.

Take I your wish I leap into the seas, where's hourly trouble for a minute's ease.

A twelvemonth longer, let me entreat you to forbear the absence of your king.

If in which time expired, he not return I shall with aged patience bear your yoke; but if I cannot win you to this love, go search like nobles, like noble subjects.

And in your search spend your adventurous worth, whom if you find and win unto return, you shall like diamonds sit about his crown.

First Lord: To wisdom he's a fool that will not yield and since Lord Helicane enjoineth us, we with our travels will endeavour us.

Helicanus: Then you love us, we you, and we'll clasp hands.

When peers thus knit, a kingdom ever stands.

(Exeunt)

Act II, Scene 5

A room in the palace. (Pentapolis)

(Simonides enters reading a letter, at one door the Knights meet him)

First Knight: Good morrow to the good Simonides.

Simonides: Knights, from my daughter this I let you know that for this twelvemonth she'll not undertake a married life.

Her reason to herself is only known, which yet from her by no means can I get.

Second Knight: May we not get access to her, my lord?

Simonides: In faith, by no means she has so strictly tied her to her chamber, that it is impossible.

One twelve moons more she'll wear Diana's livery, this by the eye of Cynthia hath she vowed, and on her virgin honour will not break it.

Third Knight: Loath to bid farewell, we take our leaves.

(Exeunt Knights)

Simonides: So, they are well dispatched; now to my daughter's letter.

She tells me here, she'd wed the stranger knight, or never more to view nor day nor light.

It is well mistress; your choice agrees with mine; I like that well.

Nay, how absolute she's in it, not minding whether I dislike or no!

Well, I do commend her choice and will no longer have it be delayed.

Soft! Here he comes, I must dissemble it.

(Pericles enters)

Pericles: All fortune to the good Simonides!

Simonides: To you as much, sir! I am beholding to you for your sweet music this last night.

I do protest my ears were never better fed with such delightful pleasing harmony.

Pericles: It is your grace's pleasure to commend; not my desert.

Simonides: Sir, you are music's master.

Pericles: The worst of all her scholars, my good lord.

Simonides: Let me ask you one thing.

What do you think of my daughter, sir?

Pericles: A most virtuous princess.

Simonides: And she is fair too, is she not?

Pericles: As a fair day in summer, wondrous fair.

Simonides: Sir, my daughter thinks very well of you; ay, so well that you must be her master, and she will be your scholar; therefore look to it.

Pericles: I am unworthy for her schoolmaster.

Simonides: She thinks not so; peruse this writing else.

Pericles: (From Aside) What's here?

A letter, that she loves the knight of Tyre! It is the king's subtlety to have my life.

Oh seek not to entrap me, gracious lord, a stranger and distressed gentleman that never aimed so high to love your daughter, but bent all offices to honour her.

Simonides: Thou hast bewitched my daughter, and thou art a villain.

Pericles: By the gods, I have not.

Never did thought of mine levy offence, nor never did my actions yet commence a deed might gain her love or your displeasure.

Simonides: Traitor, thou liest.

Pericles: Traitor!

Simonides: Ay, traitor.

Pericles: Even in his throat, unless it be the king, that calls me traitor, I return the lie.

Simonides: (From Aside) Now, by the gods, I do applaud his courage.

Pericles: My actions are as noble as my thoughts, that never relished of a base descent.

I came unto your court for honour's cause, and not to be a rebel to her state; and he that otherwise accounts of me; this sword shall prove he's honour's enemy.

Simonides: No? Here comes my daughter, she can witness it.

(Thaisa enter)

Pericles: Then, as you are as virtuous as fair, resolve your angry father, if my tongue did were solicit, or my hand subscribe to any syllable that made love to you.

Thaisa: Why, sir, say if you had, who takes offence at that would make me glad?

Simonides: Yea, mistress, are you so peremptory?

(From Aside)

I am glad on it with all my heart.

I'll tame you, I'll bring you in subjection.

Will you, not having my consent, bestow your love and your affections upon a stranger?

(From Aside)

Who, for aught I know, may be, nor can I think the contrary as great in blood as I myself; therefore hear you, mistress.

Either frame your will to mine, and you sir, hear you either be ruled by me, or I will make you man and wife.

Nay, come, your hands and lips must seal it too, and being joined I'll thus your hopes destroy; and for a further grief, God give you joy!

What, are you both pleased?

Thaisa: Yes, if you love me, sir.

Pericles: Even as my life, or blood that fosters it.

Simonides: What, are you both agreed?

Both: Yes, if it please your majesty.

Simonides: It pleaseth me so well; that I will see you wed and then with what haste you can get you to bed.

(Exeunt)

Act III, Intro

(Gower enters)

Gower: Now sleep y-slaked hath the rout; no din but snores the house about made louder by the over-fed breast of this most pompous marriage-feast.

The cat, with eyes of burning coal now crouches before the mouse's hole, and crickets sing at the oven's mouth; ever the blither for their drouth.

Hymen hath brought the bride to bed, where by the loss of maidenhead a babe is moulded.

Be attentive, and time that is so briefly spent with your fine fancies quaintly echo.

What's dumb in show I'll plain with speech.

(Pericles and Simonides enter at one door with Attendants, a Messenger meets them, kneels, and gives Pericles a letter)

(Pericles shows letter to Simonides, the Lords kneel to him)

(Thaisa who is with child is accompanied by Lychorida who is a nurse.

(The King shows her the letter; she rejoices)

(She and Pericles takes leave of her father, and depart with Lychorida and their Attendants, then exeunt Simonides and the rest)

By many a dern and painful perch of Pericles the careful search, by the four opposing coigns, which the world together joins is made with all due diligence that horse and sail and high expense can stead the quest.

At last from Tyre, fame answering the most strange inquire to the court of King Simonides are letters brought, the tenor these.

Antiochus and his daughter dead, the men of Tyrus on the head of Helicanus would set on the crown of Tyre, but he will none.

The mutiny he there hastes it oppress says to them, if King Pericles come not home in twice six moons; he, obedient to their dooms will take the crown.

The sum of this brought hither to Pentapolis, you ravished the regions round, and every one with claps can sound.

Our heir-apparent is a king! Who dreamed, who thought of such a thing?'

Brief, he must hence depart to Tyre.

His queen with child makes her desire, which who shall cross? Along to go.

Omit we all their dole and woe.

Lychorida, her nurse, she takes and so to sea.

Their vessel shakes on Neptune's billow, half the flood hath their keel cut, but fortune's mood varies again; the grisly north disgorges such a tempest forth as a duck for life that dives, so up and down the poor ship drives.

The lady shrieks, and well-a-near does fall in travail with her fear, and what ensues in this fell storm shall for itself, itself perform.

I nill relate, action may conveniently the rest convey, which might not what by me is told.

In your imagination hold this stage the ship, upon whose deck the sea-tost Pericles appears to speak.

(Exits)

Act III, Scene 1

On ship.

(Pericles enters on shipboard)

Pericles: Thou god of this great vast, rebuke these surges, which wash both heaven and hell; and thou, that hast upon the winds command, bind them in brass having called them from the deep!

Oh still, thy deafening, dreadful thunders, gently quench thy nimble, sulphurous flashes!

Oh how, Lychorida, how does my queen?

Thou stormest venomously, wilt thou spit all thyself?

The seaman's whistle is as a whisper in the ears of death, unheard.

Lychorida!

Lucina, Oh divinest patroness, and midwife gentle to those that cry by night, convey thy deity aboard our dancing boat; make swift the pangs of my queen's travails!

(Lychorida enters with an Infant)

Now, Lychorida!

Lychorida: Here is a thing too young for such a place, who if it had conceit would die, as I am like to do.

Take in your arms this piece of your dead queen.

Pericles: How, how, Lychorida!

Lychorida: Patience, good sir; do not assist the storm.

Here's all that is left living of your queen, a little daughter.

For the sake of it, be manly and take comfort.

Pericles: Oh you gods! Why do you make us love your goodly gifts, and snatch them straight away?

We here below recall not what we give, and therein may use honour with you.

Lychorida: Patience, good sir, even for this charge.

Pericles: Now, mild may be thy life! For a more blustrous birth had never babe.

Quiet and gentle thy conditions! For thou art the rudeliest welcome to this world that ever was prince's child.

Happy what follows!

Thou hast as chiding a nativity as fire, air, water, earth, and heaven can make, to herald thee from the womb.

Even at the first thy loss is more than can thy portage quit, with all thou canst find here.

Now, the good gods throw their best eyes upon it!

(Two Sailors enter)

First Sailor: What courage, sir? God save you!

Pericles: Courage enough, I do not fear the flaw; it hath done to me the worst.

Yet, for the love of this poor infant, this fresh-new sea-farer, I would it would be quiet.

First Sailor: Slack the bolins there! Thou wilt not, wilt thou?

Blow, and split thyself.

Second Sailor: But sea-room and the brine and cloudy billow kiss the moon, I care not.

First Sailor: Sir, your queen must overboard: the sea works high, the wind is loud, and will not lie till the ship be cleared of the dead.

Pericles: That's your superstition.

First Sailor: Pardon us, sir; with us at sea it hath been still observed, and we are strong in custom; therefore briefly yield her for she must overboard straight.

Pericles: As you think meet. Most wretched queen!

Lychorida: Here she lies, sir.

Pericles: A terrible childbed hast thou had, my dear; no light, no fire.

The unfriendly elements forgot thee utterly.

Nor have I time to give thee hallowed to thy grave, but straight must cast thee, scarcely coffined, in the ooze where for a monument upon thy bones; and ever-remaining lamps, the belching whale and humming water must overwhelm thy corpse lying with simple shells.

Oh Lychorida, bid Nestor bring me spices, ink and paper, my casket and my jewels; and bid Nicander bring me the satin coffer.

Lay the babe upon the pillow, quicken thee whiles I say a priestly farewell to her.

Suddenly, woman.

(Lychorida exits)

Second Sailor: Sir, we have a chest beneath the hatches, caulked and bitumed ready.

Pericles: I thank thee. Mariner, say what coast is this?

Second Sailor: We are near Tarsus.

Pericles: Thither, gentle mariner, alter thy course for Tyre.

When canst thou reach it?

Second Sailor: By break of day, if the wind cease.

Pericles: Oh make for Tarsus!

There will I visit Cleon, for the babe cannot hold out to Tyrus; there I'll leave it at careful nursing.

Go thy ways, good mariner, I'll bring the body presently.

(Exeunt)

Act III, Scene 2

A room in Cerimon's house. (Ephesus)

(Cerimon enters with a Servant, and some Persons whohave been shipwrecked)

Cerimon: Philemon, oh!

(Philemon enters)

Philemon: Doth my lord call?

Cerimon: Get fire and meat for these poor men, it has been a turbulent and stormy night.

Servant: I have been in many; but such a night as this, till now, I never endured.

Cerimon: Your master will be dead ere you return, there's nothing can be ministered to nature that can recover him.

(To Philemon)

Give this to the pothecary, and tell me how it works.

(Exeunt all but Cerimon)

(Two Gentlemen enter)

First Gentleman: Good morrow.

Second Gentleman: Good morrow to your lordship.

Cerimon: Gentlemen, why do you stir so early?

First Gentleman: Sir, our lodgings, standing bleak upon the sea; shook as the earth did quake.

The very principals did seem to rend and all-to topple: pure surprise and fear made me to quit the house.

Second Gentleman: That is the cause we trouble you so early, it is not our husbandry.

Cerimon: Oh you say well.

First Gentleman: I much marvel that your lordship, having rich tire about you, should at these early hours shake off the golden slumber of repose.

It is most strange, nature should be so conversant with pain being thereto not compelled.

Cerimon: I hold it ever, virtue and cunning were endowments greater than nobleness and riches.

Careless heirs may the two latter darken and expend, but immortality attends the former.

Making a man a god, it is known, I ever have studied physic; through which secret art.

By turning over authorities I have together with my practise, made familiar to me and to my aid the blest infusions that dwell in vegetables, in metals, stones, and I can speak of the disturbances that nature works; and of her cures which doth give me a more content in course of true delight, than to be thirsty after tottering honour, or tie my treasure up in silken bags to please the fool and death.

Second Gentleman: Your honour has through Ephesus poured forth your charity, and hundreds call themselves your creatures who by you have been restored; and not your knowledge, your personal pain, but even your purse still open hath built Lord Cerimon such strong renown as time shall never decay.

(Two or three Servants enter with a chest)

First Servant: Lift there.

Cerimon: What is that?

First Servant: Sir, even now did the sea toss upon our shore this chest.

It is of some wreck.

Cerimon: Set it down, let's look upon it.

Second Gentleman: It is like a coffin, sir.

Cerimon: Whatever it be, it is wondrous heavy.

Wrench it open straight if the sea's stomach be overcharged with gold, it is a good constraint of fortune it belches upon us.

Second Gentleman: It is so, my lord.

Cerimon: How close it is caulked and bitumed!

Did the sea cast it up?

First Servant: I never saw so huge a billow, sir, as tossed it upon shore.

Cerimon: Wrench it open;

Soft! It smells most sweetly in my sense.

Second Gentleman: A delicate odour.

Cerimon: As ever hit my nostril. So, up with it. 1360

Oh you most potent gods! Wwhat's here? A corpse!

First Gentleman: Most strange!

Cerimon: Shrouded in cloth of state balmed and entreasured with full bags of spices!

A passport too!

Apollo, perfect me in the characters!

(Reads from a scroll)

Here I give to understand, if ever this coffin drive a-land; I King Pericles, have lost this queen, worth all our mundane cost.

Who finds her, give her burying; she was the daughter of a king.

Besides this treasure for a fee, the gods requite his charity!

If thou livest, Pericles, thou hast a heart that even cracks for woe! This chanced tonight.

Second Gentleman: Most likely, sir.

Cerimon: Nay, certainly to-night, for look how fresh she looks!

They were too rough that threw her in the sea.

Make a fire within, fetch hither all my boxes in my closet.

(A Servant exits)

Death may usurp on nature many hours, and yet the fire of life kindle again the overpressed spirits.

I heard of an Egyptian that had nine hours lien dead who was by good appliance recovered.

(A Servant re-enters with boxes, napkins, and fire)

Well said, well said; the fire and cloths.

The rough and woeful music that we have cause it to sound, beseech you.

The viol once more: how thou stirr'st, thou block!

The music there! I pray you, give her air.

Gentlemen, this queen will live; nature awakes a warmth breathes out of her.

She hath not been entranced above five hours, see how she gins to blow into life's flower again!

First Gentleman: The heavens, through you, increase our wonder and set up your fame forever.

Cerimon: She is alive, behold, her eyelids, cases to those heavenly jewels which Pericles hath lost begin to part their fringes of bright gold.

The diamonds of a most praised water do appear, to make the world twice rich.

Live and make us weep to hear your fate, fair creature; rare as you seem to be.

(She moves)

Thaisa: Oh dear Diana,

Where am I? Where's my lord? What world is this?

Second Gentleman: Is not this strange?

First Gentleman: Most rare.

Cerimon: Hush, my gentle neighbours!

Lend me your hands; to the next chamber bear her.

Get linen, now this matter must be looked to, for her relapse is mortal.

Come, come and Aesculapius guide us!

(Exeunt, carrying her away)

Act III, Scene 3

A room in Cleon's house. (Tarsus)

(Pericles, Cleon, Dionyza, and Lychorida with Marina in her arms enter)

Pericles: Most honoured Cleon, I must needs be gone…

My twelve months are expired, and Tyrus stands in a litigious peace.

You, and your lady, take from my heart all thankfulness!

The gods make up the rest upon you!

Cleon: Your shafts of fortune, though they hurt you mortally, yet glance full wanderingly on us.

Dionyza: Oh your sweet queen!

That the strict fates had pleased you had brought her hither, to have blessed mine eyes with her!

Pericles: We cannot but obey the powers above us.

Could I rage and roar as doth the sea she lies in, yet the end must be as it is.

My gentle babe Marina, whom for she was born at sea; I have named so.

Here I charge your charity withal, leaving her the infant of your care, beseeching you to give her princely training, that she may be mannered as she is born.

Cleon: Fear not, my lord, but think your grace that fed my country with your corn for which the people's prayers still fall upon you; must in your child be thought on.

If neglection should therein make me vile, the common body by you relieved, would force me to my duty, but if to that my nature need a spur the gods revenge it upon me and mine to the end of generation!

Pericles: I believe you, your honour and your goodness teach me to it, without your vows.

Till she be married, madam, by bright Diana whom we honour, all unscissor'd shall this hair of mine remain, though I show ill in it.

So I take my leave, good madam, make me blessed in your care in bringing up my child.

Dionyza: I have one myself, who shall not be more dear to my respect than yours, my lord.

Pericles: Madam, my thanks and prayers.

Cleon: We'll bring your grace even to the edge on the shore, than give you up to the masked Neptune and the gentlest winds of heaven.

Pericles: I will embrace your offer.

Come, dearest madam.

Oh no tears, Lychorida, no tears.

Look to your little mistress, on whose grace you may depend hereafter.

Come, my lord.

(Exeunt)

Act III, Scene 4

A room in Cerimon's house. (Ephesus)

(Cerimon and Thaisa enter)

Cerimon: Madam, this letter, and some certain jewels, lay with you in your coffer; which are now at your command.

Know you the character?

Thaisa: It is my lord's.

That I was shipped at sea, I well remember even on my yarning time; but whether there delivered, by the holy gods, I cannot rightly say.

Since King Pericles, my wedded lord, I never shall see again a vestal livery will I take me to, and never more have joy.

Cerimon: Madam, if this you purpose as ye speak, Diana's temple is not distant far where you may abide till your date expire.

Moreover, if you please, a niece of mine shall there attend you.

Thaisa: My recompense is thanks, that's all, yet my good will is great; though the gift small.

(Exeunt)

Act IV, Intro

(Gower enters)

Gower: Imagine Pericles arrived at Tyre, welcomed and settled to his own desire.

His woeful queen we leave at Ephesus unto Diana there a votaress.

Now to Marina bend your mind whom our fast-growing scene must find at Tarsus, and by Cleon trained in music, letters; who hath gained of education all the grace, which makes her both the heart and place of general wonder.

Alas that monster envy often the wrack of earned praise, Marina's life seeks to take off by treason's knife, and in this kind hath our Cleon one daughter, and a wench full grown, even ripe for marriage-rite; this maid Hight Philoten.

It is said for certain in our story, she would ever with Marina be.

Be it when she weaved the sleided silk with fingers long, small, white as milk; or when she would with sharp needle wound the cambric, which she made more sound by hurting it; or when to the lute she sung and made the night-bird mute that still records with moan.

Or when she would with rich and constant pen Vail to her mistress Dian, still this Philoten contends in skill with absolute Marina.

So with the dove of Paphos might the crow life feathers white.

Marina gets all praises, which are paid as debts, and not as given.

This so darks in Philoten all graceful marks, that Cleon's wife, with envy rare, a present murderer does prepare for good Marina, that her daughter might stand peerless by this slaughter.

The sooner her vile thoughts to stead, Lychorida, our nurse is dead.

Cursed Dionyza hath the pregnant instrument of wrath pressed for this blow

The unborn event I do commend to your content, only I carry winged time post on the lame feet of my rhyme; which never could I so convey unless your thoughts went on my way.

Dionyza does appear with Leonine, a murderer.

(Exits)

Act IV, Scene 1

An open place near the sea-shore. (Tarsus)

(Dionyza and Leonine enter)

Dionyza: Thy oath remember, thou hast sworn to do it.

It is but a blow, which never shall be known.

Thou canst not do a thing in the world so soon to yield thee so much profit.

Let not conscience, which is but cold inflaming love in thy bosom, inflame too nicely; nor let pity, which even women have cast off, melt thee, but be a soldier to thy purpose.

Leonine: I will do it; but yet she is a goodly creature.

Dionyza: The fitter, then, the gods should have her.

Here she comes weeping for her only mistress' death.

Thou art resolved?

Leonine: I am resolved.

(Marina enters with a basket of flowers)

Marina: No, I will rob Tellus of her weed, to strew thy green with flowers.

The yellows, blues, the purple violets, and marigolds shall as a carpet hang upon thy grave; while summer-days do last.

Ay me! poor maid born in a tempest, when my mother died this world to me is like a lasting storm whirring me from my friends.

Dionyza: How now, Marina! Why do you keep alone?

How chance my daughter is not with you? Do not consume your blood with sorrowing: you have A nurse of me.

Lord, how your favour's changed with this unprofitable woe!

Come, give me your flowers, were the sea mar it.

Walk with Leonine, the air is quick there and it pierces and sharpens the stomach.

Come Leonine, take her by the arm, walk with her.

Marina: No, I pray you, I'll not bereave you of your servant.

Dionyza: Come, come, I love the king your father, and yourself; with more than foreign heart.

We every day expect him here when he shall come and find our paragon to all reports thus blasted; he will repent the breadth of his great voyage.

Blame both my lord and me, that we have taken no care to your best courses.

Go, I pray you, walk and be cheerful once again; reserve that excellent complexion which did steal the eyes of young and old.

Care not for me, I can go home alone.

Marina: Well, I will go but yet I have no desire to it.

Dionyza: Come, come, I know it is good for you.

Walk half an hour, Leonine, at the least.

Remember what I have said.

Leonine: I warrant you, madam.

Dionyza: I'll leave you, my sweet lady, for a while.

Pray, walk softly, do not heat your blood.

What! I must have a care of you.

Marina: My thanks, sweet madam.

(Dionyza exits)

Is this wind westerly that blows?

Leonine: South-west.

Marina: When I was born, the wind was north.

Leonine: Was it so?

Marina: My father, as nurse said, did never fear but cried: Good seaman!

To the sailors, galling his kingly hands, haling ropes; and clasping to the steer, endured a sea that almost burst the deck.

Leonine: When was this?

Marina: When I was born.

Never was waves nor wind more violent and from the ladder-tackle washes off a canvas-climber.

Ha!' says one, 'wilt out?'

And with a dropping industry they skip from stem to stern: the boatswain whistles, and the master calls, and trebles their confusion.

Leonine: Come, say your prayers.

Marina: What mean you?

Leonine: If you require a little space for prayer, I grant it.

Pray, but be not tedious, for the gods are quick of ear and I am sworn to do my work with haste.

Marina: Why will you kill me?

Leonine: To satisfy my lady.

Marina: Why would she have me killed?

Now, as I can remember, by my troth, I never did her hurt in all my life.

I never spoke bad words, nor did ill turn to any living creature; believe me; there, I never killed a mouse, nor hurt a fly.

I trod upon a worm against my will, but I wept for it.

How have I offended, wherein my death might yield her any profit, or my life imply her any danger?

Leonine: My commission is not to reason of the deed; but do it.

Marina: You will not do it for all the world, I hope.

You are well favoured and your looks foreshow; you have a gentle heart.

I saw you lately when you caught hurt in parting two that fought.

Good sooth, it showed well in you, do so now your lady seeks my life; come you between and save poor me, the weaker.

Leonine: I am sworn, and will dispatch.

(He seizes her)

(Pirates enters)

First Pirate: Hold, villain!

(Leonine runs away)

Second Pirater: A prize! A prize!

Third Pirate: Half-part, mates, half-part.

Come, let's have her aboard suddenly.

(Exeunt Pirates with Marina)

(Leonine re-enters)

Leonine: These roguing thieves serve the great pirate Valdes and they have seized

Marina: Let her go, there's no hope she will return.

I'll swear she's dead, and thrown into the sea; but I'll see further.

Perhaps they will but please themselves upon her, not carry her aboard.

If she remain whom they have ravished must by me be slain.

(Exits)

Act IV, Scene 2

A room in a brothel. (Mytilene)

(Pandar, Bawd, and Boult enter)

Pandar: Boult!

Boult: Sir?

Pandar: Search the market narrowly, Mytilene is full of gallants.

We lost too much money this mart by being too wenchless.

Bawd: We were never so much out of creatures.

We have but poor three, and they can do no more than they can do; and they with continual action are even as good as rotten.

Pandar: Therefore let's have fresh ones, whatever we pay for them.

If there be not a conscience to be used in every trade, we shall never prosper.

Bawd: Thou sayest true.

It is not our bringing up of poor bastards, as I think I have brought up some eleven…

Boult: Ay to eleven, and brought them down again; but shall I search the market?

Bawd: What else, man? The stuff we have, a strong wind will blow it to pieces, they are so pitifully sodden.

Pandar: Thou sayest true; they're too unwholesome, of conscience. The poor Transylvanian is dead, that lay with the little baggage.

Boult: Ay, she quickly pooped him, she made him roast-meat for worms, but I'll go search the market.

(Exits)

Pandar: Three or four thousand chequins were as pretty a proportion to live quietly, and so give over.

Bawd: Why to give over, I pray you? Is it a shame to get when we are old?

Pandar: Oh our credit comes not in like the commodity, nor the commodity wages not with the danger, therefore, if in our youths we could pick up some pretty estate; it were not amiss to keep our door hatched.

Besides, the sore terms we stand upon with the gods will be strong with us for giving over.

Bawd: Come, other sorts offend as well as we.

Pandar: As well as we! Ay, and better too; we offend worse.

Neither is our profession any trade, it's no calling; but here comes Boult.

(Boult re-enters with the Pirates and Marina)

Boult: (To Marina) Come your ways.

My masters, you say she's a virgin?

First Pirate: Oh sir, we doubt it not.

Boult: Master, I have gone through for this piece, you see.

If you like her, so; if not, I have lost my earnest.

Bawd: Boult, has she any qualities?

Boult: She has a good face, speaks well, and has excellent good clothes.

There's no further necessity of qualities can make her be refused.

Bawd: What's her price, Boult?

Boult: I cannot be bated one doit of a thousand pieces.

Pandar: Well, follow me, my masters, you shall have your money presently.

Wife, take her in; instruct her what she has to do, that she may not be raw in her entertainment.

(Exeunt Pandar and Pirates)

Bawd: Boult, take you the marks of her, the colour of her hair, complexion, height, age, with warrant of her virginity; and cry: he that will give most shall have her first.

Such a maidenhead were no cheap thing, if men were as they have been.

Get this done as I command you.

Boult: Performance shall follow.

(Exits)

Marina: Alack that Leonine was so slack, so slow!

He should have struck, not spoke; or that these pirates,

Not enough barbarous, had not o'erboard thrown me

For to seek my mother!

Bawd: Why lament you, pretty one?

Marina: That I am pretty.

Bawd: Come, the gods have done their part in you.

Marina: I accuse them not.

Bawd: You are light into my hands, where you are like to live.

Marina: The more my fault to escape his hands where I was like to die.

Bawd: Ay, and you shall live in pleasure.

Marina: No.

Bawd: Yes, indeed shall you, and taste gentlemen of all fashions.

You shall fare well, you shall have the difference of all complexions.

What! do you stop your ears?

Marina: Are you a woman?

Bawd: What would you have me be, and I be not a woman?

Marina: An honest woman, or not a woman.

Bawd: Marry, whip thee, gosling.

I think I shall have something to do with you.

Come, you're a young foolish sapling, and must be bowed as I would have you.

Marina: The gods defend me!

Bawd: If it please the gods to defend you by men, then men must comfort you, men must feed you, men must stir you up.

Boult's returned.

(Boult re-enters)

Now, sir, hast thou cried her through the market?

Boult: I have cried her almost to the number of her hairs, I have drawn her picture with my voice.

Bawd: And I pray to thee, tell me, how dost thou find the inclination of the people, especially of the younger sort?

Boult: It faith, they listened to me as they would have hearkened to their father's testament.

There was a spaniard's mouth so watered, that he went to bed to her very description.

Bawd: We shall have him here to-morrow with his best ruff on.

Boult: To-night, to-night. But, mistress, do you know the French knight that cowers in the hams?

Bawd: Who, Monsieur Veroles?

Boult: Ay, he: he offered to cut a caper at the proclamation, but he made a groan at it and swore he would see her to-morrow.

Bawd: Well, well; as for him, he brought his disease hither.

Here he does but repair it.

I know he will come in our shadow to scatter his crowns in the sun.

Boult: Well, if we had of every nation a traveller, we should lodge them with this sign.

Bawd: (To Marina) Pray you, come hither awhile.

You have fortunes coming upon you.

Mark me, you must seem to do that fearfully which you commit willingly, despise profit where you have most gain.

To weep that you live as ye do makes pity in your lovers seldom, but that pity begets you a good opinion, and that opinion a mere profit.

Marina: I understand you not.

Boult: Oh take her home, mistress, take her home.

These blushes of hers must be quenched with some present practise.

Bawd: Thou sayest true in faith, so they must for your bride goes to that with shame, which is her way to go with warrant.

Boult: With faith some do, and some do not; but mistress, if I have bargained for the joint…

Bawd: Thou mayst cut a morsel off the spit.

Boult: I may so.

Bawd: Who should deny it? Come, young one, I like the manner of your garments well.

Boult: Ay, by my faith, they shall not be changed yet.

Bawd: Boult, spend thou that in the town: report what a sojourner we have, you'll lose nothing by custom.

When nature flamed this piece, she meant thee a good turn, therefore say what a paragon she is, and thou hast the harvest out of thine own report.

Boult: I warrant you, mistress, thunder shall not so awake the beds of eels as my giving out her beauty stir up the lewdly-inclined.

I'll bring home some to-night.

Bawd: Come your ways; follow me.

Marina: If fires be hot, knives sharp, or waters deep, untied I still my virgin knot will keep.

Diana, aid my purpose!

Bawd: What have we to do with Diana? Pray you, will you go with us?

(Exeunt)

Act IV, Scene 3

A room in Cleon's house. (Tarsus)

(Cleon and Dionyza enter)

Dionyza: Why, are you foolish? Can it be undone?

Cleon: Oh Dionyza, such a piece of slaughter the sun and moon ne'er looked upon!

Dionyza: I think you'll turn a child again.

Cleon: Were I chief lord of all this spacious world, I would give it to undo the deed.

O lady, much less in blood than virtue, yet a princess to equal any single crown on the earth in the justice of compare!

Oh villain Leonine! Whom thou hast poisoned too.

If thou hadst drunk to him, it had been a kindness becoming well thy fact.

What canst thou say when noble Pericles shall demand his child?

Dionyza: That she is dead.

Nurses are not the fates to foster it, nor ever to preserve.

She died at night, I'll say so.

Who can cross it?

Unless you play the pious innocent and for an honest attribute cry out: she died by foul play.'

Cleon: Oh go to.

Well, well, of all the faults beneath the heavens, the gods do like this worst.

Dionyza: Be one of those that think the petty wrens of Tarsus will fly hence, and open this to Pericles; I do shame to think of what a noble strain you are and of how coward a spirit.

Cleon: To such proceeding whoever but his approbation added, though not his prime consent, he did not flow from honourable sources.

Dionyza: Be it so, then, yet none does know but you how she came dead, nor none can know; Leonine being gone.

She did disdain my child, and stood between her and her fortunes.

None would look on her, but cast their gazes on Marina's face whilst ours was blurted at and held a making not worth the time of day.

It pierced me through, and though you call my course unnatural, you not your child well loving; yet I find it greets me as an enterprise of kindness performed to your sole daughter.

Cleon: Heavens forgive it!

Dionyza: And as for Pericles, what should he say?

We wept after her hearse, and yet we mourn.

Her monument is almost finished and her epitaphs in glittering golden characters express a general praise to her, and care in us at whose expense it is done.

Cleon: Thou art like the harpy, which to betray dost with thine angel's face seize with thine eagle's talons.

Dionyza: You are like one that superstitiously doth swear to the gods that winter kills the flies; but yet I know you'll do as I advise.

(Exeunt)

Act IV, Scene 4

Chorus.

(Gower enters before the monument of Marina at Tarsus)

Gower: Thus time we waste, and longest leagues make short sail seas in cockles, have and wish but for it; making to take your imagination from bourn to bourn, region to region.

By you being pardoned, we commit no crime to use one language in each several clime, where our scenes seem to live.

I do beseech you to learn of me, who stand in the gaps to teach you the stages of our story.

Pericles is now again thwarting the wayward seas, attended on by many a lord and knight.

To see his daughter, as she is all his life's delight, old Escanes, whom Helicanus late advanced in time to great and high estate, is left to govern.

Bear you it in mind, Old Helicanus goes along behind.

Well-sailing ships and bounteous winds have brought this king to Tarsus, think his pilot thought; so with his steerage shall your thoughts grow on to fetch his daughter home, who first is gone.

Like motes and shadows see them move awhile; your ears unto your eyes I'll reconcile.

(Pericles enters at one door with all his entourage, Cleon and Dionyza, at the other)

(Cleon shows Pericles the tomb whereat Pericles makes lamentation, puts on sackcloth, and in a mighty passion departs)

(Exeunt Cleon and Dionyza)

See how belief may suffer by foul show!

This borrowed passion stands for true old woe, and Pericles in sorrow all devoured, with sighs shot through, and biggest tears overshowered, leaves Tarsus and again embarks.

He swears never to wash his face, nor cut his hairs.

He puts on sackcloth, and to sea, he bears a tempest which his mortal vessel tears, and yet he rides it out.

Now please you wit and the epitaph is for Marina writ by wicked Dionyza.

(Reads the inscription on Marina's monument)

The fairest, sweet'st, and best lies here, who withered in her spring of year.

She was of Tyrus the king's daughter, on whom foul death hath made this slaughter; Marina was she called, and at her birth, Thetis, being proud swallowed some part on the earth.

Therefore the earth, fearing to be overflowed, hath Thetis' birth-child on the heavens bestowed.

Wherefore she does, and swears she'll never stint, make raging battery upon shores of flint.

No visor does become black villany so well as soft and tender flattery.

Let Pericles believe his daughter's dead, and bear his courses to be ordered by Lady Fortune, while our scene must play his daughter's woe and heavy well-a-day in her unholy service.

Patience then, and think you now are all in Mytilene.

(Exits)

Act IV, Scene 5

A street before the brothel. (Mytilene)

(Two Gentlemen enter from the brothel)

First Gentleman: Did you ever hear the like?

Second Gentleman: No, nor never shall do in such a place as this, she being once gone.

First Gentleman: But to have divinity preached there! Did you ever dream of such a thing?

Second Gentleman: No, no. Come, I am for no more bawdy-houses. Shall we go hear the vestals sing?

First Gentleman: I'll do anything now that is virtuous, but I am out of the road of rutting for ever.

(Exeunt)

Act IV, Scene 6

A room in the brothel.

(Pandar, Bawd, and Boult enter)

Pandar: Well, I had rather than twice the worth of her she had never come here.

Bawd: Fie, fie upon her! She's able to freeze the god Priapus, and undo a whole generation.

We must either get her ravished, or be rid of her.

When she should do for clients her fitment, and do me the kindness of our profession, she has me her quirks, her reasons, her master reasons, her prayers, her knees; that she would make a puritan of the devil if he should cheapen a kiss of her.

Boult: In faith I must ravish her, or she'll disfurnish us of all our cavaliers, and make our swearers priests.

Pandar: Now, the pox upon her green-sickness for me!

Bawd: With faith, there's no way to be rid on it but by the way to the pox.

Here comes the Lord Lysimachus disguised.

Boult: We should have both lord and jester, if the peevish baggage would but give way to customers.

(Lysimachus enters)

Lysimachus: How now! How a dozen of virginities?

Bawd: Now, the gods to-bless your honour!

Boult: I am glad to see your honour in good health.

Lysimachus: You may so, it is the better for you that your resorters stand upon sound legs.

How now! Wholesome iniquity have you that a man may deal withal, and defy the surgeon?

Bawd: We have here one, sir, if she would, but there never came her like in Mytilene.

Lysimachus: If she would do the deed of darkness, thou wouldst say.

Bawd: Your honour knows what it is to say well enough.

Lysimachus: Well, call forth, call forth.

Boult: For flesh and blood, sir, white and red, you shall see a rose; and she were a rose indeed, if she had but…

Lysimachus: What, pray to thee?

Boult: Oh sir, I can be modest.

Lysimachus: That dignifies the renown of a bawd, no less than it gives a good report to a number to be chaste.

(Boult exits)

Bawd: Here comes that which grows to the stalk never plucked yet, I can assure you.

(Boult with **Marina re-enter)**

Is she not a fair creature?

Lysimachus: 'Faith, she would serve after a long voyage at sea.

Well, there's for you, leave us.

Bawd: I beseech your honour, give me leave: a word, and I'll have done presently.

Lysimachus: I beseech you, do.

Bawd: (To Marina) First, I would have you note, this is an honourable man.

Marina: I desire to find him so, that I may worthily note him.

Bawd: Next, he's the governor of this country, and a man whom I am bound to.

Marina: If he govern the country, you are bound to him indeed, but how honourable he is in that, I know not.

Bawd: Pray you, without any more virginal fencing, will you use him kindly?

He will line your apron with gold.

Marina: What he will do graciously, I will thankfully receive.

Lysimachus: Have you done?

Bawd: My lord, she's not paced yet, you must take some pains to work her to your manage.

Come, we will leave his honour and her together.

Go thy ways.

(Exeunt Bawd, Pandar, and Boult)

Lysimachus: Now, pretty one, how long have you been at this trade?

Marina: What trade, sir?

Lysimachus: Why, I cannot name't but I shall offend.

Marina: I cannot be offended with my trade. Please you to name it.

Lysimachus: How long have you been of this profession?

Marina: Ever since I can remember.

Lysimachus: Did you go to it so young?

Were you a gamester at five or at seven?

Marina: Earlier too, sir, if now I be one.

Lysimachus: Why, the house you dwell in proclaims you to be a creature of sale.

Marina: Do you know this house to be a place of such resort, and will come into it?

I hear say you are of honourable parts, and are the governor of this place.

Lysimachus: Why, hath your principal made known unto you who I am?

Marina: Who is my principal?

Lysimachus: Why, your herb-woman; she that sets seeds and roots of shame and iniquity.

Oh you have heard something of my power, and so stand aloof for more serious wooing, but I protest to thee, pretty one, my authority shall not see thee, or else look friendly upon thee.

Come, bring me to some private place.

Come, come.

Marina: If you were born to honour, show it now;

If put upon you, make the judgment good

That thought you worthy of it.

Lysimachus: How's this? How's this? Some more; be sage.

Marina: For me that am a maid, though most ungentle fortune have placed me in this sty, where, since I came; diseases have been sold dearer than physic.

Oh that the gods would set me free from this unhallowed place, though they did change me to the meanest bird that flies in the purer air!

Lysimachus: I did not think thou couldst have spoke so well; never dreamed thou couldst.

Had I brought hither a corrupted mind, thy speech had altered it.

Hold, here's gold for thee.

Persever in that clear way thou goest and the gods strengthen thee!

Marina: The good gods preserve you!

Lysimachus: For me, be you thoughten that I came with no ill intent for to me the very doors and windows savour vilely.

Fare thee well.

Thou art a piece of virtue, and I doubt not but thy training hath been noble.

Hold, here's more gold for thee.

A curse upon him, die he like a thief that robs thee of thy goodness!

If thou dost hear from me, it shall be for thy good.

(Boult re-enters)

Boult: I beseech your honour, one piece for me.

Lysimachus: Avaunt, thou damned door-keeper!

Your house, but for this virgin that doth prop it, would sink and overwhelm you. Away!

(Exits)

Boult: How's this? We must take another course with you.

If your peevish chastity, which is not worth a breakfast in the cheapest country under the cope, shall undo a whole household, let me be gelded like a spaniel.

Come your ways.

Marina: Whither would you have me?

Boult: I must have your maidenhead taken off, or the common hangman shall execute it.

Come your ways.

We'll have no more gentlemen driven away.

Come your ways, I say.

(Bawd re-enters)

Bawd: How now! What's the matter?

Boult: Worse and worse, mistress; she has here spoken holy words to the Lord Lysimachus.

Bawd: Oh abominable!

Boult: She makes our profession as it were to stink afore the face of the gods.

Bawd: Marry, hang her up for ever!

Boult: The nobleman would have dealt with her like a nobleman, and she sent him away as cold as a snowball; saying his prayers too.

Bawd: Boult, take her away; use her at thy pleasure crack the glass of her virginity, and make the rest malleable.

Boult: An if she were a thornier piece of ground than she is, she shall be ploughed.

Marina: Hark, hark, you gods!

Bawd: She conjures: away with her! Would she had never come within my doors!

Merrily hang you! She's born to undo us.

Will you not go the way of women-kind?

Merrily, come up, my dish of chastity with rosemary and bays!

(Exits)

Boult: Come, mistress; come your ways with me.

Marina: Whither wilt thou have me?

Boult: To take from you the jewel you hold so dear.

Marina: Pray I to thee, tell me one thing first.

Boult: Come now, your one thing.

Marina: What canst thou wish thine enemy to be?

Boult: Why, I could wish him to be my master, or rather, my mistress.

Marina: Neither of these are so bad as thou art, since they do better thee in their command.

Thou hold'st a place, for which the pained'st fiend of hell would not in reputation change:

Thou art the damned doorkeeper to every Coistrel that comes inquiring for his Tib.

To the choleric fisting of every rogue, thy ear is liable; thy food is such as hath been belched on by infected lungs.

Boult: What would you have me do? Go to the wars, would you?

Where a man may serve seven years for the loss of a leg, and have not money enough in the end to buy him a wooden one?

Marina: Do anything but this thou doest.

Empty, old receptacles, or common shores, of filth; serve by indenture to the common hangman.

Any of these ways are yet better than this, for what thou professest a baboon, could he speak, would own a name too dear.

Oh that the gods would safely deliver me from this place!

Here, here's gold for thee.

If that thy master would gain by thee, proclaim that I can sing, weave, sew, and dance with other virtues; which I'll keep from boast, and I will undertake all these to teach.

I doubt not but this populous city will yield many scholars.

Boult: But can you teach all this you speak of?

Marina: Prove that I cannot, take me home again and prostitute me to the basest groom that doth frequent your house.

Boult: Well, I will see what I can do for thee.

If I can place thee, I will.

Marina: But amongst honest women.

Boult: In faith, my acquaintance lies little amongst them, but since my master and mistress have bought you, there's no going but by their consent; therefore I will make them acquainted with your purpose, and I doubt not but I shall find them tractable enough.

Come, I'll do for thee what I can; come your ways.

(Exeunt)

Act V, Intro

(Gower enters)

Gower: Marina thus the brothel escapes, and chances into an honest house, our story says.

She sings like one immortal, and she dances as goddess-like to her admired lays; deep clerks she dumbs; and with her needle composes nature's own shape, of bud, bird, branch, or berry, that even her art sisters the natural roses; her inkle, silk, twin with the rubied cherry.

That pupils lacks she none of noble race, who pour their bounty on her, and her gain is she gives the cursed bawd.

Here we her place, and to her father turn our thoughts again where we left him, on the sea.

We there him lost; whence driven before the winds he is arrived here where his daughter dwells; and on this coast suppose him now at anchor.

The city strived, God Neptune's annual feast to keep from whence Lysimachus our Tyrian ship espies; his banners sable, trimmed with rich expense and to him in his barge with fervor his.

In your supposing once more put your sight of heavy Pericles; think this his bark.

Where what is done in action more if might shall be discovered, if it please you sit and hark.

(Exits)

Act V, Scene 1

On board Pericles' ship, off Mytilene.

(Pavilion on deck with a curtain before it; Pericles within it is reclined on a couch)

(A barge lying beside the Tyrian vessel.

(Two Sailors enter, one belonging to the Tyrian vessel, the other to the barge; to them Helicanus)

Tyrian Sailor: (To the Sailor of Mytilene) Where is lord Helicanus?

He can resolve you.

Oh here he is.

Sir, there's a barge put off from Mytilene, and in it is Lysimachus the governor who craves to come aboard.

What is your will?

Helicanus: That he have his. Call up some gentlemen.

Tyrian Sailor: Oh gentlemen! My lord calls.

(Two or three Gentlemen enter)

First Gentleman: Doth your lordship call?

Helicanus: Gentlemen, there's some of worth would come aboard; I pray ye; greet them fairly.

(The Gentlemen and the two Sailors descend, and go on board the barge)

(From thence Lysimachus and Lords enter with the Gentlemen and the two Sailors)

Tyrian Sailor: Sir, this is the man that can, in aught you would resolve you.

Lysimachus: Hail, reverend sir! The gods preserve you!

Helicanus: And you, sir, to outlive the age I am, and die as I would do.

Lysimachus: You wish me well.

Being on shore, honouring of Neptune's triumphs, seeing this goodly vessel ride before us,

I made to it, to know of whence you are.

Helicanus: First, what is your place?

Lysimachus: I am the governor of this place you lie before.

Helicanus: Sir, our vessel is of Tyre, in it the king; a man who for this three months hath not spoken to anyone, nor taken sustenance but to prorogue his grief.

Lysimachus: Upon what ground is his distemperature?

Helicanus: It would be too tedious to repeat, but the main grief springs from the loss of a beloved daughter and a wife.

Lysimachus: May we not see him?

Helicanus: You may, but bootless is your sight, he will not speak to any.

Lysimachus: Yet let me obtain my wish.

Helicanus: Behold him.

(Pericles is discovered)

This was a goodly person till the disaster that, one mortal night, drove him to this.

Lysimachus: Sir king, all hail! The gods preserve you!

Hail, royal sir!

Helicanus: It is in vain, he will not speak to you.

First Lord: Sir, we have a maid in Mytilene, I durst wager would win some words of him.

Lysimachus: It is well me-thought.

She questionless with her sweet harmony and other chosen attractions would allure, and make a battery through his deafened parts, which now are midway stopped.

She is all happy as the fairest of all, and with her fellow maids is now upon the leafy shelter that abuts against the island's side.

(Whispers a Lord, who goes off in the barge of Lysimachus)

Helicanus: Sure, all's affectless, yet nothing we'll omit that bears recovery's name; but, since your kindness we have stretched thus far, let us beseech you that for our gold we may provision have, wherein we are not destitute for want, but weary for the staleness.

Lysimachus: Oh sir, a courtesy which if we should deny, the most just gods for every mistake would send a caterpillar onto a butterfly, onto a typhoon and tidal wave, and so afflict our province.

Yet once more, let me entreat to know at large the cause of your king's sorrow.

Helicanus: Sit, sir, I will recount it to you, but see, I am prevented.

(Lord, with Marina, and a young Lady re-enters from the barge)

Lysimachus: Oh here is the lady that I sent for.

Welcome, fair one!

Is it not a goodly presence?

Helicanus: She's a gallant lady.

Lysimachus: She's such a one, that, were I well assured came of a gentle kind and noble stock, I would wish no better choice, and think me rarely wed.

Fair one, all goodness that consists in bounty expect even here, where is a kingly patient.

If that thy prosperous and artificial feat can draw him but to answer thee in aught, thy sacred physic shall receive such pay as thy desires can wish.

Marina: Sir, I will use my utmost skill in his recovery, provided that none but I and my companion maid be suffered to come near him.

Lysimachus: Come, let us leave her, and the gods make her prosperous!

(Marina sings)

Lysimachus: Marked he your music?

Marina: No, nor looked on us.

Lysimachus: See, she will speak to him.

Marina: Hail, sir! My lord, lend ear.

Pericles: Hum, ha!

Marina: I am a maid, my lord, that ne'er before invited eyes, but have been gazed on like a comet.

She speaks, my lord that may be hath endured a grief might equal yours, if both were justly weighed.

Though wayward fortune did malign my state, my derivation was from ancestors who stood equivalent with mighty kings, but time hath rooted out my parentage and to the world and awkward casualties bound me in servitude.

(From Aside)

I will desist, but there is something glows upon my cheek and whispers in mine ear: go not till he speak.

Pericles: My fortunes, parentage, good parenting to equal mine!

Was it not thus? What say you?

Marina: I said, my lord, if you did know my parenting.

You would not do me violence.

Pericles: I do think so.

Pray you, turn your eyes upon me.

You are like something that, what country-woman? Here of these shores?

Marina: No, nor of any shores.

Yet I was mortally brought forth, and am no other than I appear.

Pericles: I am great with woe, and shall deliver weeping.

My dearest wife was like this maid, and such a one my daughter might have been my queen's square brows; her stature to an inch as wand-like straight.

As silver-voiced her eyes as jewel-like and cased as richly in pace to another Juno who starves the ears she feeds, and makes them hungry the more she gives them speech.

Where do you live?

Marina: Where I am but a stranger from the deck, you may discern the place.

Pericles: Where were you bred?

How achieved you these endowments, which you make more rich to owe?

Marina: If I should tell my history, it would seem like lies disdained in the reporting.

Pericles: Pray I to thee, speak.

Falseness cannot come from thee, for thou look'st as modest as Justice, and thou seem'st a palace for the crowned truth to dwell in.

I will believe thee, and make my senses credit thy relation to points that seem impossible; for thou look'st like one I loved indeed.

What were thy friends? Didst thou not say, when I did push thee back which was when I perceived thee, that thou camest from good descending?

Marina: So indeed I did.

Pericles: Report thy parenting.

I think thou said'st thou hadst been tossed from wrong to injury, and that thou thought'st thy griefs might equal mine; if both were opened.

Marina: Some such thing I said, and said no more but what my thoughts did warrant me was likely.

Pericles: Tell thy story, if thine considered prove the thousandth part of my endurance, thou art a man, and I have suffered like a girl.

Yet thou dost look like Patience gazing on kings' graves, and smiling extremity out of act.

What were thy friends? How lost thou them?

Thy name, my most kind virgin?

Recount, I do beseech thee: come, sit by me.

Marina: My name is Marina.

Pericles: Oh I am mocked and thou by some incensed god sent hither to make the world to laugh at me.

Marina: Patience, good sir, or here I'll cease.

Pericles: Nay, I'll be patient.

Thou little know'st how thou dost startle me, to call thyself Marina.

Marina: The name was given me by one that had some power, my father and he is a king.

Pericles: How! A king's daughter? And called Marina?

Marina: You said you would believe me, but not to be a troubler of your peace, I will end here.

Pericles: But are you flesh and blood?

Have you a working pulse? And are no fairy?

Motion well, speak on, where were you born? And wherefore called Marina?

Marina: Called Marina for I was born at sea.

Pericles: At sea! What mother?

Marina: My mother was the daughter of a king who died the minute I was born, as my good nurse Lychorida hath often deliver'd weeping.

Pericles: Oh stop there a little!

(From Aside)

This is the rarest dream that ever dull sleep, did mock sad fools withal.

This cannot be, my daughter's buried.

Well, where were you bred? I'll hear you more to the bottom of your story and never interrupt you.

Marina: You scorn; believe me, it were best I did give over.

Pericles: I will believe you by the syllable of what you shall deliver.

Yet, give me leave, how came you in these parts?

Where were you bred?

Marina: The king my father did in Tarsus leave me till cruel Cleon, with his wicked wife, did seek to murder me.

And having woo'd a villain to attempt it, who having drawn to do it, a crew of pirates came and rescued me; brought me to Mytilene, but good sir, whither will you have me?

Why do you weep? It may be, you think me an impostor.

No, good faith, I am the daughter to King Pericles, If good King Pericles be.

Pericles: Ho, Helicanus!

Helicanus: Calls my lord?

Pericles: Thou art a grave and noble counsellor, most wise in general.

Tell me, if thou canst, what this maid is, or what is like to be, that thus hath made me weep?

Helicanus: I know not, but here is the regent sir of Mytilene who speaks nobly of her.

Lysimachus: She would never tell her parenting, being demanded that she would sit still and weep.

Pericles: Oh Helicanus strike me honoured sir; give me a gash, put me to present pain lest this great sea of joys rushing upon me overbear the shores of my mortality and drown me with their sweetness.

Oh come hither, thou that beget'st him that did thee beget, thou that was it born at sea, buried at Tarsus, and found at sea again!

Oh Helicanus, down on thy knees thank the holy gods as loud as thunder threatens us.

This is Marina.

What was thy mother's name? Tell me but that, for truth can never be confirmed enough, though doubts did ever sleep.

Marina: First, sir, I pray what is your title?

Pericles: I am Pericles of Tyre, but tell me now my drown'e queen's name, as in the rest you said thou hast been godlike perfect, the heir of kingdoms and another like to Pericles thy father.

Marina: Is it no more to be your daughter than to say my mother's name was Thaisa?

Thaisa was my mother, who did end the minute I began.

Pericles: Now, blessing on thee! Rise, thou art my child.

Give me fresh garments. Mine own, Helicanus, she is not dead at Tarsus as she should have been by savage Cleon.

She shall tell thee all when thou shalt kneel, and justify in knowledge she is thy very princess.

Who is this?

Helicanus: Sir, it is the governor of Mytilene who, hearing of your melancholy state, did come to see you.

Pericles: I embrace you.

Give me my robes, I am wild in my beholding.

Oh heavens bless my girl! But, hark, what music?

Tell Helicanus, my Marina, tell him over, point by point, for yet he seems to doubt; how sure you are my daughter, but what music?

Helicanus: My lord, I hear none.

Pericles: None!

The music of the spheres! List, my Marina.

Lysimachus: It is not good to cross him, give him way.

Pericles: Rarest sounds! Do ye not hear?

Lysimachus: My lord, I hear.

(Music)

Pericles: Most heavenly music!

It nips me unto listening, and thick slumber hangs upon mine eyes.

Let me rest.

(Sleeps)

Lysimachus: A pillow for his head.

So leave him all.

Well, my companion friends, if this but answer to my just belief I'll well remember you.

(Exeunt all but Pericles)

(Diana appears to Pericles as in a vision)

Diana: My temple stands in Ephesus: quicken thee thither, and do upon mine altar sacrifice.

There, when my maiden priests are met together, before the people all reveal how thou at sea didst lose thy wife.

To mourn thy crosses, with thy daughter's, call and give them repetition to the life or perform my bidding, or thou livest in woe; do it and be happy by my silver bow!

Awake, and tell thy dream.

(Disappears)

Pericles: Celestial Dian, goddess argentine,

I will obey thee. Helicanus!

(Helicanus, Lysimachus, and Marina re-enter)

Helicanus: Sir?

Pericles: My purpose was for Tarsus, there to strike the inhospitable Cleon; but I am for other service first.

Toward Ephesus, turn our blown sails; lefts soon, I'll tell thee why.

(To Lysimachus)

Shall we refresh us, sir, upon your shore and give you gold for such provision as our intents will need?

Lysimachus: Sir, with all my heart and when you come ashore I have another suit.

Pericles: You shall prevail, were it to woo my daughter; for it seems you have been noble towards her.

Lysimachus: Sir, lend me your arm.

Pericles: Come, my Marina.

(Exeunt)

Act V, Scene 2

Chorus.

(Gower enters before the temple of Diana at Ephesus)

Gower: Now our sands are almost run, more a little and then dumb.

This, my last boon, give me, for such kindness must relieve me that you aptly will suppose.

What pageantry, what feats, what shows, what minstrelsy and pretty din the regent made in Mytilene to greet the king.

So he thrived, that he is promised to be wived to fair Marina, but in no wise till he had done his sacrifice, as Dian bade.

Whereto being bound, the interim, pray you, all confound.

In feathered briefness sails are filled, and wishes fall out as they're willed.

At Ephesus, the temple sees our king and all his company.

That he can hither come so soon, is by your fancy's thankful doom.

(Exits)

Act V, Scene 3

The temple of Diana at Ephesus.

(Thaisa standing near the altar as high priestess, a number of Virgins on each side, with Cerimon and other Inhabitants of Ephesus attending)

(Pericles enters with his entourage, Lysimachus, Helicanus, Marina, and a Lady enter)

Pericles: Hail Dian! To perform thy just command, I here confess myself the king of Tyre; who frighted from my country did wed at Pentapolis the fair Thaisa.

At sea in childbed died she, but brought forth a maid-child called Marina, who, O goddess wears yet thy silver livery.

She at Tarsus was nursed with Cleon, who at fourteen years he sought to murder, but her better stars brought her to Mytilene, her fortunes brought the maid aboard us; where by her own most clear remembrance she made known herself my daughter.

Thaisa: Voice and favour!

You are, you are, oh royal Pericles!

(Faints)

Pericles: What means the nun? She dies! Help, gentlemen!

Cerimon: Noble sir, if you have told Diana's altar true, this is your wife.

Pericles: Reverend appearer no; I threw her overboard with these very arms.

Cerimon: Upon this coast, I warrant you.

Pericles: It is most certain.

Cerimon: Look to the lady, oh she's but overjoyed.

Early in blustering morn this lady was thrown upon this shore.

I opened the coffin, found there rich jewels, recovered her and placed her here in Diana's temple.

Pericles: May we see them?

Cerimon: Great sir, they shall be brought you to my house, whither I invite you.

Look, Thaisa is recovered.

Thaisa: Oh let me look!

If he be none of mine, my sanctity will to my sense bend no licentious ear, but curb it, spite of seeing.

Oh my lord, are you not Pericles? Like him you spake, like him you are.

Did you not name a tempest a birth and death?

Pericles: The voice of dead Thaisa!

Thaisa: That Thaisa am I, supposed dead and drowned.

Pericles: Immortal Dian!

Thaisa: Now I know you better.

When we with tears parted Pentapolis, the king my father gave you such a ring.

(Shows a ring)

Pericles: This, this.

No more you gods! Your present kindness makes my past miseries sports.

You shall do well, that on the touching of her lips I may melt and no more be seen.

Oh come, be buried a second time within these arms.

Marina: My heart leaps to be gone into my mother's bosom.

(Kneels to Thaisa)

Pericles: Look, who kneels here! Flesh of thy flesh, Thaisa; thy burden at the sea, and called Marina, for she was yielded there.

Thaisa: Blest, and mine own!

Helicanus: Hail, madam, and my queen!

Thaisa: I know you not.

Pericles: You have heard me say, when I did fly from Tyre, I left behind an ancient substitute.

Can you remember what I called the man?

I have named him often.

Thaisa: It was Helicanus then.

Pericles: Still confirmation; embrace him dear Thaisa, this is he.

Now do I long to hear how you were found; how possibly preserved, and who to thank, besides the gods for this great miracle.

Thaisa: Lord Cerimon, my lord, this man through whom the gods have shown their power that can from first to last resolve you.

Pericles: Reverend sir, the gods can have no mortal officer more like a god than you.

Will you deliver how this dead queen re-lives?

Cerimon: I will, my lord.

Beseech you, first go with me to my house where shall be shown you all was found with her, how she came placed here in the temple; no needful thing omitted.

Pericles: Pure Dian, bless thee for thy vision!

I will offer night-oblations to thee.

Thaisa, this prince, the fair-betrothed of your daughter shall marry her at Pentapolis.

And now, this ornament makes me look dismal, will I clip to form; and what this fourteen years no razor touched to grace thy marriage-day, I'll beautify.

Thaisa: Lord Cerimon hath letters of good credit, sir, my father's dead.

Pericles: Heavens make a star of him! Yet there, my queen, we'll celebrate their nuptials, and ourselves will in that kingdom spend our following days.

Our son and daughter shall in Tyrus reign.

Lord Cerimon, we do our longing stay to hear the rest untold.

Sir, lead us the way.

(Exeunt)

(Gower enters)

Gower: In Antiochus and his daughter you have heard of monstrous lust the due and just reward.

In Pericles, his queen and daughter, seen although assailed with fortune fierce and keen, virtue preserved from fell destruction's blast, led on by heaven and crowned with joy at last.

In Helicanus may you well descry a figure of truth, of faith, of loyalty.

In reverend Cerimon there well appears the worth that learned charity aye wears.

For wicked Cleon and his wife, when fame had spread their cursed deed, and honoured name f Pericles, to rage the city turn, that him and his they in his palace burn.

The gods for murder seemed so content to punish them, although not done but meant.

So, on your patience evermore attending,

New joy wait on you! Here our play has ending.

(Exits)

The End

Description of Titles

The Comedy of Errors
Caught in a land of embittered woman and war, caught in months of strife, where a merchant's visit offers little natural relief. The fleeting moment of approving gold, inspire further bitterness, upon an approach to the marketplace, and then the women that occupy within them.

19 Characters

The Taming of the Shrew
Arrangements are made to spencer would be suiters to melt the splendors of a strong willed women. The winning is found pledged, influencing maids to seek their turns, and meanwhile terms required, an authentic spirit that they will/would wed soon.

34 Characters

Love's Labor's Lost
The house of a scholarly pursuit, returns into an expressive, either poetic or drunken as highlighting the gold-slur filled house of charms and dance like rhymes

19 Characters

A Midsummer Night's Dream
Journey into a land of fairies, where creatures are found to have the same issues as nobilities. Exemplifying, perhaps, there's no place like home. Meet fairies as they frolic and play the noble hearts and sway, posed in the recesses of night, and mystic lands of a faraway kingdom.

22 Characters

The Merchant of Venice

An angry Shylock brings to trial a merchant, over a lover's quarrel disrupted, demanding pounds of flesh. With no desires for even three times the amount, the Shylock demands his vengeance at heart.

22 Characters

The Merry Wives of Windsor
Mistresses and lords try and relate towards one another, as various important community figures come to have their word/seek the hostesses. Pleasantries are exchanged as a range of charms are expressed, until conversation resembled so to folly.

23 Characters

Much Ado About Nothing
Soldiery level consideration occupy the gossip, as several hostilities are summoned up, onto heart related matter. Also in conflict. The latter portion of the story lightens up to a women's home and pleasantries. Thereafter, a general search and care in actions, creating response phrasing poetic to the responses of leadership parading, until an end full of sensitivity asking gently questions, onto kisses

23 Characters

As You Like It
Troubled lower nobles venture about daily business, with some mild graces towards the ladies found. In need of relief or play, the Duke and family members take to the woods, where jests of drinking turn into troubled amusements, or warmth of a women's heart.

26 Characters

Troilus and Cressida
The infamous Greek battle for Troy. A large army arrives to take back the lost love of a humiliated foe. Both sides mobilize heroes onto the field, as soldiers and generals move to the side, and let strategies and fate take their course.

21+ Characters

All's Well That Ends Well
A tale of delightful, womanly gossip of a prestigious sort, until the French King has his word on the excellence of others. The story initially revolves around a strong willed countess, whose courteous pose and insight, reflect a nobility reflective of the house and court (council). Dialogue therein revolving around the councils rather, to exemplify (court counselling women).

25 Characters

Measure for Measure
Statesmen discourse leading with time to a personal reflection. Strolling Dukes and strong willed women occupy the background, where high-function status and family discourse intertwine within formalities (of administrative foresight, expression) observed.

24 Characters

Richard III
An in palace drama with King Richard the 3rd, Queen Elizabeth, and Queen Margret. Onto a haunting reunion, as the state processes royal executions.

61+ Characters

The Life and Death of King John
King John and Queen Elinor entertain the royal court, where a bastard has come to make his day. Strategic deployments of influence are exemplified, as the bastard plots about until alerts, alarm corruption has delivered trouble makers known.

24 Characters

Romeo and Juliet
Lovers emerge within a city gripped with two feuding houses apposed. As turmoil are caught in bitter heat, the lover's. Bliss and undying pledge becomes them, onto the eternal soul (of love and romance).

33 Characters

Othello
A hopeful Othello calls upon the favor of allies based on proposed merits, which called upon allies and foes to him. In a mixed response, allies and foes campaign both against Othello, becoming a bitter, personal tangle over a mislead love adventure representing the future of either fates

25 Characters

Macbeth
A desperate Macbeth ventures towards witches to tell fortune, returning to a castle haunted by ghost/old-spirits. Macbeth's worries become frightful nightmares, along the despair of the household around him.

39 Characters

Mark Antony and Cleopatra

The relations or affections of Mark Anthony and Cleopatra, onto the strategic interactions between Mark Anthony and Octavius. The discourse moves to the Octavius house, revealing Octavia, and later then, Pompey in the background. Overall the focus retains upon Mark Anthony, Cleopatra, and Octavius.

56+ Characters

Coriolanus

Citizens riot during a famine, while the state administrative intervenes and otherwise discourses the seriousness of the matter and war. Lady's calm the general ambience, until the sword is mobilized to defend the gates, , while the plight of people is nevertheless heard convincing Roman elites the problem is being found/fought within.

60 Characters

Pericles Prince of Tyre

A thoughtful/reflective Pericles interposes his good will and well-meaning nature, which leads him to visit fishermen friends, and onto state function. Pericles is then confronted, required to (take a plunge) to marry, embedding him deeper into ocean stock of sea life among sailors experience and merchant owners, investing his interest as babe, securing his destiny as then, future king

44 Characters

Cymbeline

Cymbeline, friend or loyalist to the first Caesars, is summoned into battle. Meanwhile there are personal matters to attend to within the noble house.

41 Characters

The Winter's Tale
A gossipy tale of high office, administrative daily insight onto the tender meaning of things and people an how they unite unwittingly at the discourse of their respected hierarchies of partnership. Profoundness therein inspiring the recounts of clown and child, as examples perhaps of what state administration and or nobility's company keeps.

34+ Characters

The Tempest
After an earth shattering storm, a fairy dwelling world is found. There magic and graces are there in song, glory and praises.

21 Characters

The Two Gentlemen of Verona
Loving beginnings, yet far too. General virtues going upwards in hierarchies, with overall chivalrous wits.

Twelfth Night
An evening in the company of sound gatherings, seemingly a docile manner recount version of noble delights. In similarities of the pose, composing an environment of insight and oversight.

Henry the 8th
Across chamber and palace, Dukes and lords, until Queen Katharine's and King Henry VIII's present their graces, conversing the Cardinal then. The signs then, an Elizabeth is born.

Richard II
King Richard the 2nd readies the armed forces at the sound of alarm, while later Henry IV is near for discussion. King Richard the 2nd and his groom.

Henry V
King Henry the 5th, as found across his palace, until a readiness for war. King Henry the 5th and the French King, with armies both have at it.

Henry VI, Part 1
Funeral of King Henry the 5th, Henry VI makes his approach to France. Henry VI fashions as thy lord protector.

Henry VI, Part 2
King Henry the 6th, where the Cardinal is seen mocking protectors with praise, as all the rage. Queen Margaret at King Henry VI, until the end.

Henry VI, Part 3
King Henry VI is busy fighting a succession of battles, France and England as having at it, yet again.

King Henry the 5th
King Henry 5 fight his way toward France, they reach the peaceful and loving responses of a French King.

Henry IV, Part 1
King Henry the 4th, from Palace to Pub, onto the battle fields again. Until there is no rebellion.

Henry IV, Part 2
Henry IV, from Palace, Priest and then tavern, he nevertheless finds some peace, after reflection. King Henry IV, and then King Henry V as fashionable by the end.

Titus Andronicus
A story of Romans and Goths, where roman sways give way. And then to see about Goths and proving worthiness.

28 Characters

Julius Caesar
Near the Final days of the 1st Caesar, and the continuation everlasting as through Octavius.

Hamlet
Hamlet, and his father the King, the father yet a Ghost. Hamlet, not so eager to join.

King Lear
King Lear, from palace to castle, to fighting the French in the field. After battle King Lear is in bed, the Doctor discourses, what lays then now, will have an impact upon the end.

Timon of Athens
A story set in Greece, a place of poets and cultured, good graces. From Arts and daily expressive, to political and charmed.

www.ingramcontent.com/pod-product-compliance
Lightning Source LLC
Chambersburg PA
CBHW071503080526
44587CB00014B/2201